MEXICO
Major highways, missions, archaeological zones

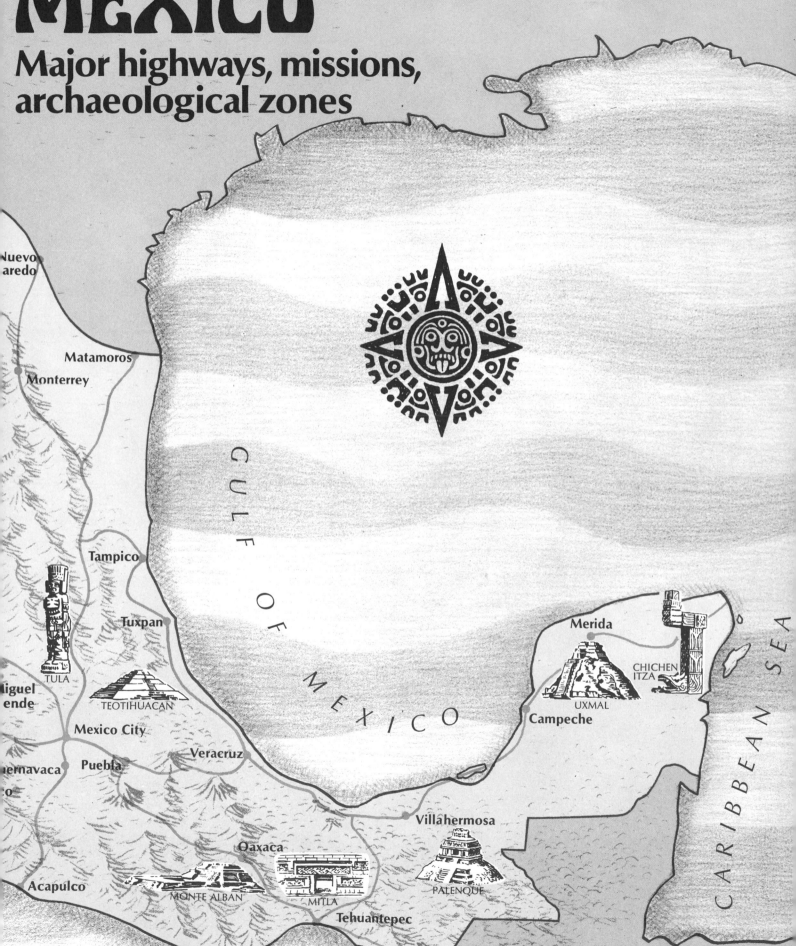

Nuevo Laredo

Matamoros

Monterrey

GULF OF MEXICO

Tampico

Tuxpan

TULA

Miguel ende

TEOTIHUACAN

Mexico City

Cuernavaca

Puebla

Veracruz

Acapulco

Oaxaca

MONTE ALBAN

MITLA

Tehuantepec

Villahermosa

PALENQUE

Merida

UXMAL

CHICHEN ITZA

Campeche

CARIBBEAN SEA

LANE MAGAZINE & BOOK COMPANY

A Sunset Pictorial

MEXICO

MENLO PARK, CALIFORNIA

Mexico

Edited by Jack McDowell

Design and Layout: Henry Rasmussen
Illustrations and Cartography: Amado Gonzalez

Consultants: Pauline R. Kibbe, Virginia B. de Barrios
Editorial Minutiae Mexicana, Mexico City

Travel Editor, Sunset Magazine: Larry Smith
Executive Editor, Sunset Books: David E. Clark

PHOTOGRAPHERS

GUILLERMO ALDANA: 84; 121 right. WILLIAM APLIN: 38 all; 39 bottom. CAROL ANN BALES: 85. BANCROFT LIBRARY: 18 right. KEN BATES: 35 bottom; 37. JON BRENNEIS: 81 bottom left, center, right. J. Y. BRYAN: 21 top left; 40; 41 all; 48 all; 49 all; 106; 107; 108; 109 all; 112; 119 all. CASASOLA: 28 left, bottom right. GLENN CHRISTIANSEN: 32; 34; 35 top; 36; 46; 52. BRAD COOPER: 171 top. DICK DAVIS: 190; 246 right; 251. EASTERN AIRLINES: 164. RICHARD ELKUS: 47. CARLOS ELMER: 89 top. LEE FOSTER: 43 top; 127 bottom left; 212 center. FROJEN CHIPPENDALE: 101 top. ELLEN KADELBURG: 59 bottom right; 60; 61 top center, bottom; 66; 68 bottom; 72; 73; 75 right; 80 left; 82; 83; 87 right; 126 left; 151 bottom right; 186 all. KARL KERNBERGER: 113. LIBRARY OF CONGRESS: 23 right; 24 top, center; 25 left; 26 left, bottom; 27 bottom left; 28 top; 29 all. FR. ERNESTO LOERA: 56; 57 all; 58; 59 left, top right. THOMAS MAHNKEN: 33 all. MARINE CORPS MUSEUM: 23 bottom. ROSARIO MAZZEO: 88 top right. CARLOS BARRIOS MARTINEZ: 64 bottom; 65 top. JACK MCDOWELL: 7; 9; 10; 14 right; 15 top; 16 top, bottom right; 18 left; 19 left, top; 20 left, top, bottom center; 21 bottom; 22 all; 42 all; 64 top; 67; 68 top; 69; 70; 71 all; 74; 75 left; 78; 79 all; 80 right; 81 top left; 86; 87 left; 88 top left; 89 bottom; 90; 91 all; 92; 93; 96 all; 97 all; 110 all; 111 all; 120 all; 127 top left, right; 128 all; 129; 130; 131 all; 132; 133 all; 134 all; 135 all; 136 all; 137; 138 right; 139; 140 all; 141 all; 143 all; 146; 147 all; 148 all; 149 all; 150 left, top; 154; 155 all; 156 all; 157 all; 158; 159 all; 160; 161 all; 162 all; 163 all; 165 all; 166; 167; 168 all; 169 all; 170 all; 171 bottom left, right; 172 all; 173 all; 174 all; 175 right; 176; 177; 179 top; 180; 181 all; 182 all; 183 all; 184; 185 all; 187 all; 188 all; 189 all; 191; 192; 193 all; 194 right; 195 all; 198 all; 199 all; 200; 201 all; 202; 203; 204; 205 all; 206 all; 207 all; 208 all; 209; 210; 211 all; 212 left, bottom; 213 top, center right; 214; 215 all; 216; 217 left; 220; 221 all; 223 right; 224; 225; 226; 227; 230; 231; 232; 233 all; 238; 239 all; 241 top, right; 242 all; 244; 245 all; 246 left; 247 all; 249 all; 250 top; 253 all. JURGIS MOTIEKAITIS: 2-3; 44; 45 all; 50; 51; 53; 54; 55 all; 118; 122; 123 all; 124; 125. NATIONAL MUSEUM OF ANTHROPOLOGY: 15 left. NEW YORK PUBLIC LIBRARY: 17 bottom. DON NORMARK: 81 top right; 88 bottom; 175 left; 178; 179 bottom. OAS PHOTOS: 18 center; 19 bottom; 23 top left; 25 center, right; 27 center, right. FRANCOISE OLLIVIER: 248; 250 bottom. MARION PATTERSON: 61 top left, right; 194 left; 234; 235 all. PETE REDPATH: 21 top right; 43 right; 150 bottom. DICK ROWAN: 63 top; 101 bottom; 121 left. ROBERT SCHALKWIJK: 6; 16 bottom left; 20 bottom right; 94; 95; 98; 99 all; 100; 103 all; 114; 115 all; 117; 138 left; 142; 144 all; 145; 217 right; 222; 223 left; 228; 229 all; 240; 243; 151 top. STANFORD UNIVERSITY SPECIAL COLLECTIONS: 15 bottom; 17 top left, right. F. STOPPELMAN: 11; 65 bottom left; 151 top. SUTRO LIBRARY: 14 left; 26 top right. U.S. ARMY: 24 bottom. U.S. NAVY: 27 top. GEORGE WALLACE: 8; 116. DARROW WATT: 102; 126 right. WESTERN WAYS: 39 top; 65 right. KEN WHITMORE: 62 bottom.

Front Cover: Village of Zinapecuaro, state of Michoacan; photo by ROBERT SCHALKWIJK.
Back Cover: Blue glass, Guadalajara; photo by JACK MCDOWELL.

CONTENTS

Note: Maps shown in this book are intended as general locators only.

MEXICO IS A TIMELESS TRAIN OF YESTERDAYS...
It is the haunting melody of a reed flute played by a
Tarahumara whose brown skin is decorated with white
splotches for a half-Christian, half-pagan festival. It is the
warmth of morning sun on the wrinkled wattles of
turkeys dozing in a marketplace where fowl and fruit
are bartered in the same ageless manner they have been
exchanged for centuries.

. . . A CONTRADICTION OF CULTURES . . .
It is a Mixtec mother bundling on her back a slumbering
infant while clutching in her hand a bleating transistor
radio. It is a barefoot Tolucan tugging a burro past a
conservative German automobile while casting covetous
glances at a hopped-up Japanese motorcycle.

... A MELDING OF PAST, PRESENT, AND FUTURE.
It is an ultra-contemporary housing development that
contrasts but does not conflict with an Aztec ceremonial
center. It is an innovative architectural statement whose
form echoes the familiar peaks of eternal mountain
tops, outreaches the summits of timeworn pyramids, and
points the way to an unknown but exciting tomorrow.

Early

A Rich Heritage Born

MEXICO'S EARLIEST CULTURES are a confused mix of times, places, and natural divinities. The courses are turbulent, sometimes blending, sometimes running at cross currents to one another. New discoveries constantly challenge established dates and threaten the whole structure of the pyramid of time that represents the comfortable chronology of early Mesoamerica.

Ancient man in Mexico was a nomad until he discovered an edible grass and settled down in the dry Tehuacan Valley southeast of Mexico City to cultivate it, paying homage to the forces of nature that blessed his crops.

From out of the steaming swamps of southern Mexico and Central America arose an advanced culture that came to be called Maya. Developing about the same time in the eastern lowlands were the Olmecs, a mysterious group that—like the Maya—considered the snake and jaguar sacred beings. Chronicles of the Zapotecs in Oaxaca, a people who appeared far to the west, claimed that they had descended from the jaguar. The Mixtecs, who replaced the Zapotecs in Oaxaca, adopted many of the latter's customs and gods. Ancient Totonacs are also believed to have been related to the Olmecs; they appeared first in the Valley of Mexico—from which they were driven out by a warring tribe—and later in the vanilla jungles of Veracruz.

The influence of central plateau Teotihuacan was felt as far away as Guatemala. The decline of this mighty culture, one of whose gods was a feathered serpent, is believed to have been brought on by the Toltecs, a group who appeared mysteriously in central Mexico.

The Toltecs worshipped Quetzalcoatl, god of air and water, one of whose forms was as a human being with a fair skin and a beard who had left Mexico but would one day return. It was a legend that would haunt their successors, the Aztecs.

Beginnings
of a Tumultuous Past

MEXICO'S EARLY EMPIRES—WHEN, WHAT, WHERE?
Maya culture flourished in southeastern Mexico, Central America—its best known sites, Palenque, Chichen Itza (see pp. 216, 248). Olmec: southern Gulf Coast—La Venta (p. 214). Zapotec: central Oaxaca—Monte Alban (p. 224). Totonac: central Gulf Coast—El Tajin (pp. 2-3, photo). Teotihuacan: Central Plateau—Teotihuacan (p. 190). Mixtec: central Oaxaca—Mitla, Monte Alban (pp. 223, 224). Toltec: Valley of Mexico—Tula (p. 146). Aztec: Tenochtitlan—Ancient Mexico City (p. 14).

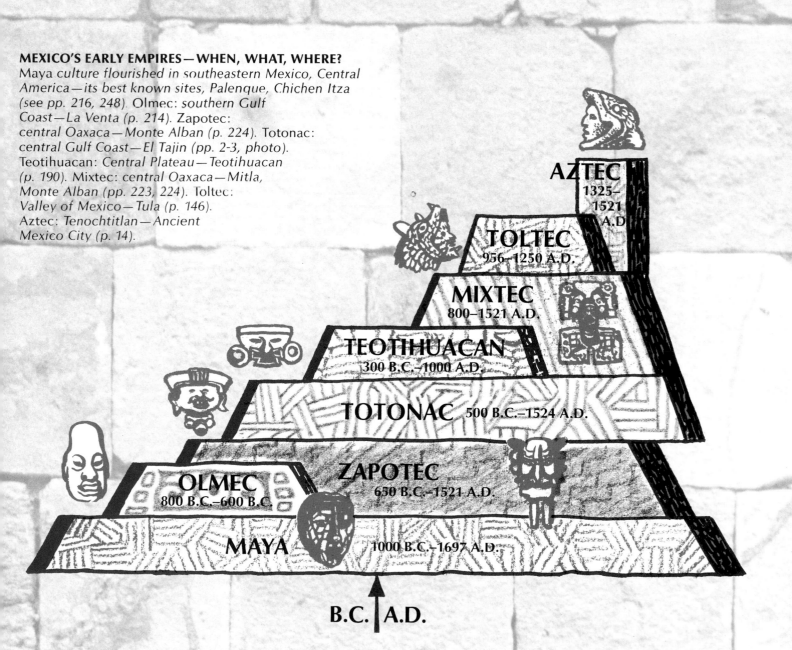

AZTEC 1325–1521 A.D

TOLTEC 956–1250 A.D.

MIXTEC 800–1521 A.D.

TEOTIHUACAN 300 B.C.–1000 A.D.

TOTONAC 500 B.C.–1524 A.D.

OLMEC 800 B.C.–600 B.C.

ZAPOTEC 650 B.C.–1521 A.D.

MAYA 1000 B.C.–1697 A.D.

B.C. A.D.

Elite Empire of the Aztecs

"The flowering of Aztec culture," writes a noted Mexican anthropologist, "was the last great event in the history of pre-Columbian Mexico." Glorious as it was, the nation of the Aztecs was a most curious one, rich in contradictions and sowing the seeds of its own destruction even while it reached full bloom. Their capital city was a model of beauty, their religion a thing of horror. They measured time more accurately than Europeans of the day but never employed the principle of the wheel. They subjugated and controlled a vast part of Mexico; yet only a few Spaniards in a strange land toppled their empire.

The Aztecs were the last of several wandering tribes that drifted into the Valley of Anahuac, now known as the Valley of Mexico, a large lake-dotted basin already populated with other tribes. Legend says that in 1325 the Aztecs established their

NATIONAL EMBLEM of Mexico is fierce eagle resting on a cactus, clutching snake in its beak. In 1325 the nomadic Aztecs came upon this sign, which had been foretold by their priests, and on that spot—an island in the middle of a large lake—established the center of their empire. Monument dramatically depicting founding of Mexico City is located at south end of capital's Zocalo, or main plaza.

home on a large island in the middle of Lake Texcoco where they witnessed an eagle devouring a snake while perched on a cactus, a sign that had been foretold by their god of war, Huitzilopochtli. A more realistic version of the founding of Tenochtitlan, as the capital was called, is that the barren, isolated chunk of land was the only place allowed them by their neighbors, who hoped they would starve to death for want of tillable soil.

But the Aztecs built *chinampas,* floating islands, by filling huge wicker baskets with soil. On these drifting plots they planted corn and trees and built huts. Eventually the *chinampas* became rooted to the shallow lake bottom and many were joined together to serve as foundations for larger structures.

Called the Venice of America, Tenochtitlan was interconnected by canals and linked to the shore by broad earth causeways that converged in the middle of the city at a large plaza. The central plaza contained a great pyramid topped by two temples, one dedicated to Huitzilopochtli, the other to Tlaloc, the rain god. There were also lesser pyramids, palaces of the chiefs, and houses for the priests. A mammoth collection of idols taken from conquered cities stood not far from a rack on which thousands of skulls of sacrificial victims were neatly arranged.

Believing that certain gods controlled rain, fire, crops, and movements of the heavenly bodies, the Aztecs strove to retain their good graces through prayers and frequent human sacrifice. Victims were held down over a stone altar while a priest ripped open the chest with an obsidian knife, tore out the heart, and offered it to images of the deities.

Prisoners of war were usually the prime choice, but there were voluntary sacrifices as well. An Aztec citizen volunteering

TENOCHTITLAN, ISLAND CAPITAL of the Aztecs, was depicted in a delightfully inaccurate map, left, published in Venice in 1556. Perhaps less fanciful, but more factual, is the model of the city's center, top right—today Mexico City's Zocalo—which forms a major exhibit in the National Museum of Anthropology. Around the shores of Lake Texcoco, and under the rule of the Aztecs, were many villages, represented in ancient Indian paintings, lower right, by curious anthropomorphic configurations.

to be a gift to the gods was richly attired and waited upon as a member of royalty for a period of one year, after which he met his death at the hands of the priests. For the devout it was the highest honor one could aspire to.

With its emphasis on the supernatural and its fear of the unknown, the Aztec religion bred superstition. The most commonplace activities were full of dreaded omens, and any untoward happening was looked upon as a fulfillment of a dire prophecy, one that demanded immediate propitiation of the gods.

Deeply embedded in the Aztec mind was the tale of Quetzalcoatl that had been passed down by the Toltecs, in which a bearded white man would come out of the east and claim their kingdom as his own.

MARKET PLACE was a bustling social nucleus for common people of Tenochtitlan, where incredible varieties of goods were exchanged. Commoners were far down on the scale of a strict caste system, right, that placed priests and warriors on top. Constant warring, slavery, and human sacrifice made life cheap, as evidenced by the symbolic altar of stone skulls.

OBSIDIAN-EDGED CLUBS were effective weapons wielded by warriors as well as by gladiatorial combatants (top left). Prisoners of the Aztecs were sometimes given the option of being sacrificial victims or fighting in public contest. Ceremonial sacrifice involved the high priest tearing out a man's heart, above, and offering it still pulsing to the gods, after which the victim's body was hurled unceremoniously down the steps of the main pyramid.

Spain Storms the New World

At the turn of the sixteenth century Spain was busily engaged in extending empire, her caravels cruising seas far away from home. After two explorations of the Mexican coast in 1517 and 1518, a third expedition was sent from Cuba in 1519 under the command of Hernan Cortes, a shrewd leader of men and a fearless soldier. Landing first at Cozumel then at Tabasco, Cortes claimed possession of the new land in the name of God and King Charles V.

Moving north to what is now Veracruz, Cortes took his men inland where word of his arrival was carried to Tenochtitlan, capital of the Aztec kingdom. After a visit by emissaries of Moctezuma, ruler of the Aztecs, Cortes sent notice that he was

...Conquest!

ROUTE OF CONQUEST
Spanish adventurers were dedicated to Cross and the Crown, motivated by expectations of riches. After a sea voyage from Cuba, a force of 663 men and 16 horses, commanded by Hernan Cortes, marched to Tenochtitlan. A peaceful occupation was short-lived. The Spanish were driven out of the city, only to return for final destruction of the capital on August 13, 1521.

Route from coast, 1519
Retreat to Tlaxcala, 1520
Return to Tenochtitlán, 1521

desirous of visiting Tenochtitlan. Fearful of the newcomers, Moctezuma attempted to dissuade them by sending gifts of gold and jewelry, which only reaffirmed Cortes' conviction that this truly was a land ripe for conquest.

On their march inland, the Spaniards were joined by Tlaxca-lans—a group of Indians from whom the Aztecs drew many serfs—who were eager to side with any attempt that might relieve them of their harsh taskmasters.

Arriving in the capital, the Spaniards were received hospitably by Moctezuma, who had decided that discretion was much the better part of valor. But Cortes took the emperor captive, claiming that he was responsible for the murder of several of his men on the coast. Moctezuma submitted to the indignity, telling the delighted Cortes that he was the one who fulfilled the ancient prophecy: "My ancestors believed that a people from whom we all descend came to this land from very far . . . then went away. They said they would return . . . to rule and command us . . . I think that it is now fulfilled . . . I regard you as our lord."

CORTES WAS AUDACIOUS, ambitious, driven by an insatiable desire for personal glory. Moctezuma was dilatory, superstitious, easily intimidated. When he realized he could neither halt nor buy off the Spaniards, he received Cortes in grandiose manner, right, virtually convinced he was a god. The woman to Cortes' right is Malinche, his Indian interpreter and traveling companion.

Being shown vast rooms full of gold and precious stones, Cortes made immediate plans for shipping the treasures back to Spain. He was interrupted, however, by the discovery of the temple of Huitzilopochtli, where he was shocked by the sight of sacrificial blood matted "two or three fingers thick" on the images of idols and the walls. Sickened, Cortes ordered destruction of the temple, to the dismay of the Aztecs.

Dismay turned to open rebellion. Moctezuma was killed, Cortes was driven out of the capital, and the Spaniards suffered terrible losses. Undaunted, Cortes retreated to Tlaxcala, where he recruited large numbers of Indian allies and prepared to return in force.

Knowing that on foot he could not carry a battle over the

waters of the lake, he had built thirteen brigantines which were then dismantled, carried in pieces to the shores of Lake Texcoco, reassembled, and launched to lay siege to the Aztec capital.

Three terrible months of warfare followed. In spite of great resistance by Cuauhtemoc, nephew of Moctezuma, the strength of the city ebbed. Resisting to the last, the people were reduced to eating worms and bark from trees until, in the words of one of the conquistadors, "God saw fit to send the Indians smallpox."

On August 13, 1521, mighty Tenochtitlan fell and a new nation and race were born.

SUCCESSOR TO MOCTEZUMA was his nephew, Cuauhtemoc, left, a noble leader of the Aztecs in their final battle against the Spaniards. In spite of defeat and torture by fire, top, he endured his sufferings and refused to reveal the whereabouts of a supposed cache of treasure. After capitulation of the Aztecs, Cortes destroyed their idols, bottom, flattened their main temple, and razed Tenochtitlan.

Colonialism: One Church-State

Even while the ruined Tenochtitlan was being rebuilt, colonizers poured into Mexico from Spain, eager to settle in a new world which they believed would offer them a life of ease. Pagan temples were destroyed and Christian churches built in their place. Indian converts were counted in the millions; it was the greatest religious conversion in history.

Since dissemination of the Catholic faith was one of the aims of the Spanish colonial system, the Church became a powerful

TRUE CONQUEST OF MEXICO was made by the missionary priests and friars who spread across the land trying to supplant paganism with Christianity. The Colonial Period was a time of church building, some modestly simple, some massively beautiful. Below, domes of Convent of San Gabriel, Cholula; upper right, Los Remedios, the church atop a pyramid, Cholula; lower left, parish church at Ozumba; lower right, church-monastery at Tepoztlan.

force in Mexico. Although padres and friars labored in the field to save souls, many of their predecessors had constructed a holy hierarchy that allowed them to acquire vast properties. At one period, half of the land and wealth of Mexico was owned by the Church, and the line between Church and State was so fine as to be undiscernible.

Reluctant to admit to Indians being their equals, the colonists set up a rigorous caste system. The aristocrats were known as *gachupines.* Pure-bloods born in Spain, they controlled the country's spiritual and political life. *Criollos,* born in Mexico of Spanish parents, were looked down upon by the *gachupines;* although capable of holding government jobs they were not allowed to. *Mestizos* were of mixed blood, half Spanish, half Indian. Excluded from most privileges and considered outcasts, they had reason to nurture revolutionary ideas.

SPANISH AND ROMAN influences are reflected in the lovely, utilitarian arches of aqueducts constructed during 16th and 17th centuries. Like many aqueducts built under the direction of Spanish engineers, those at Zacatecas (left) and Queretaro (right) are in use today.

SILVER WAS KING in Mexico in 1600 and 1700, and a handful of the country's mines more than doubled the world's entire silver supply. The Valenciana mine, still in operation in the mountains above the town of Guanajuato, is surrounded by a wall whose bold sawtooth construction was intended to duplicate and glorify in grand scale the points of the Spanish crown.

The Struggle for Independence

By 1810—some 300 years after the Conquest—Mexico's Spanish masters controlled vast tracts of land and virtually owned the people who lived on them. Fired by social injustices, a priest named Miguel Hidalgo proclaimed the day of deliverance, and with a rallying cry of "Long live our Lady of Guadalupe . . . death to the *gachupines!*" he led forth a band of insurgents.

The revolt was short-lived. Hidalgo was captured and shot, as were other leaders. Without a guiding figurehead the uprising disintegrated.

Hidalgo failed in his brave attempt to gain independence but his efforts helped to arouse a long-beleaguered people against Spanish domination.

COLONIAL CASTE SYSTEM that prevailed in Mexico had numerous ramifications, as shown in the old chart at far right. So rigid and unjust was the system that Miguel Hidalgo y Costilla, left, a parish priest, led a mob of peasants in a revolt against Spanish domination. Jose Maria Morelos, center, a follower of Hidalgo, headed the independence movement in the south. Though both men were influential early in the revolution, they and other leaders were executed.

Texas and Santa Anna's Leg

Despite the initial loss of its leaders, the insurrection moved forward, but it was not until 1821, when Colonel Agustin Iturbide took Mexico City, that Mexico realized independence. The half-century following was a confused period for Mexico. During that time the country had forty presidents, two emperors, and several provisional governments. Through the glory-loving machinations of one of its rulers, Antonio Lopez de Santa Anna (who was in and out of office eleven times), Mexico lost half of her territory.

GENERAL D. ANTONIO LOPEZ DE SANTA ANNA

VAINGLORIOUS ASPIRATIONS of Santa Anna, above left, lost Mexican territory. The American defenders of the Alamo at San Antonio, Texas, above, were wiped out in February, 1836, but U.S. was victorious at decisive battle of San Jacinto on April 21. At Monterey, California, the American flag went up on July 7, 1846, left.

Santa Anna was a soldier who had long been active in politics. He first appeared on the scene in a major way in 1829 when he led a force to Tampico to drive out a last-gasp Spanish invasionary force. A victorious hero, he overthrew the presidency and in 1833 established himself as head of Mexico.

Until then, North Americans had settled more or less peacefully in Texas, California, and the Southwest. But chafing for something to do, Santa Anna—Napoleon of the West, as he liked

NINOS HEROS, or boy heroes, were military cadets who met their death defending Mexico City's Chapultepec Castle against U.S. troops, right. Historic battle of Buenavista, below, north of Saltillo, brought disgrace to Santa Anna and glory to "Old Rough and Ready" Major General Zachary Taylor, left, below, who was elected to the U.S. Presidency in 1849.

to call himself—began to stir concern in Mexicans that their country had too many Americans in it. Convincing himself that settlers were on the verge of taking over all Mexico, he sent troops into Texas. After several skirmishes, Santa Anna himself joined battle with a group of Texans holed up in the Alamo, an abandoned mission near San Antonio. A two-week seige ended with the Americans being wiped out almost to the man.

Though a tragic loss, the fight provided northerners with a rallying cry—"Remember the Alamo!"—that gave spirit to subsequent encounters. By 1845 Texas had become part of the United States, and by 1848 all of California, Nevada, Arizona, Utah, and New Mexico had been acquired from Mexico.

Though disgraced repeatedly, Santa Anna managed to remain in the limelight. In 1838 he lost a leg defending Veracruz against French warships. By his own definition, he was once more a hero, and he never neglected to refer to the noble wound gained in defense of his country. To celebrate his birthday in 1842, "His Serene Highness" had the desiccated limb dug up and carried in grand procession to the capital, where it was enshrined with all the pomp and ceremony accorded a national hero.

Mexico's Idealistic Emperor

Of all the countries who were casting covetous eyes on Mexico during her long period of turmoil and adjustment, none was so bold as France. Confident that the United States would not interfere because it was embroiled in its own Civil War at the time, Napoleon III sent troops to Mexico, positive that a strong paternal hand would be welcomed. Suffering an initial defeat at Puebla in 1862, the French later captured the city, then took the capital, forcing President Benito Juarez to flee.

As ruler, Napoleon set up an unemployed Austrian Archduke named Maximilian, who held the throne as emperor for three years, sincerely believing all the while that he had the support of the Mexican people and of France. But in 1867 the French

MISGUIDED MAXIMILIAN and his wife Carlota, left, were enthroned as rulers of Mexico by the French, but their ill-starred reign ended in tragedy with the execution of Maximilian and Carlota's insanity. Benito Juarez, above, Mexico's counterpart of Abraham Lincoln, was a full blooded Indian who studied law and dedicated himself to justice under the law. As President of Mexico, he ousted French troops, ordered the shooting of Maximilian.

army of occupation pulled out of the country, leaving its puppet behind. Juarez returned, deposed Maximilian, and had him executed at Queretaro.

It was a pattern often repeated. Much of Mexico's turbulent early history can be summed up tersely in the words, "He was captured and shot."

Revolution! Revolution!

Distasteful though it was, the brief French interlude had one benefit. It helped to unify the people of Mexico. With the invaders gone and his country finally realizing a degree of peace, Juarez thinned out the army by releasing thousands of officers and men.

One of the disgruntled militarists who found himself at loose ends was Porfirio Diaz, a ruthless opportunist with an eye on the presidency. After the death of Juarez, Diaz quickly raised

HERO OR VILLAIN? Even today opinion is divided in Mexico regarding Porfirio Diaz, shown above as a young officer. Under the presidency of Diaz—an unprecedented 30-year dictatorship—Mexico made tremendous material progress, but at the expense of personal freedom and foreign exploitation of the country. Ownership of lavish haciendas, above right, and vast landholdings were condoned by Diaz. Francisco Madero, right, was son of a wealthy family, but his idealism caused him to become a voice for Mexico's downtrodden poor, and he headed the first social revolution.

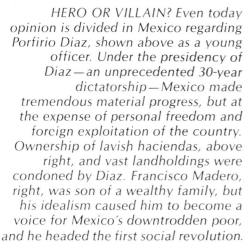

an army, proceeded into Mexico City, forced the incumbent into exile, and proclaimed himself president in 1876.

Holding Mexico in an iron hand, Diaz encouraged foreign trade and welcomed investment in the country's mines, oil deposits, and railroads. Federal income rose dramatically. The national treasury had a surplus of capital. On the surface it appeared that Mexico had at last become a progressive, democratic nation.

But Diaz stuffed the government with family and friends. To anyone who could be useful to him, he sold public lands at

EXECUTION BY FIRING SQUAD was the fate of many political prisoners and dissenters under the Diaz regime during the troubled days around the turn of the 20th century. Such acts were portents of terrible violence and bloodshed to come.

ridiculously low prices. He fragmented areas that historically had been worked by Indians, turning them into parcels of private property. By the early 1900's ninety per cent of Mexico's land was owned by less than a thousand families. One of the mightiest were the Terrazas in Chihuahua, whose holdings comprised close to 34 million acres.

Mexico was chiefly a rural country. Since the policies of Diaz were highly feudalistic, they deprived the peasant of rights to any land. Forced to buy at the hacienda store, millions of people were constantly in debt. Millions of others were impressed into outright slavery and forced to work in the jungles of Quintana Roo and Oaxaca.

For three and a half decades Porfirio Diaz held office, his

TWO REVOLUTIONARIES, and a President. Pancho Villa, far left, a one-time cattle thief and bandit, challenged federal troops and thus gathered a loyal following in the north. In the south, Emiliano Zapata, center, led peons against government forces. President Venustiano Carranza, below, was instrumental in adoption of a new Constitution, which confirmed the one promulgated in 1857 but added important changes that struck against evils of the Diaz dictatorship.

...Revolution!

THE RAILROADS played an important role during the Revolution. Not all trains completed their routes, since rebels delighted in blowing up government shipments. Though trains were excruciatingly slow and delays were numerous, riding even on the front of the locomotive was better than slogging along on foot. Soldaderas, or female soldiers, pitched tents on top of box cars, followed their men over the countryside, participated in battles.

sheer might effectively quashing dissent. Nearing the election year of 1910 at age 80, Diaz declared grandly that he would stand for re-election but would welcome political opposition. A quiet intellectual named Francisco I. Madero took Diaz at his word and announced that he would be a candidate. He was promptly jailed.

With Diaz once more in office, Madero was released. Immediately he declared the election unconstitutional and called for an uprising. Two men from the north were the first to respond: Pascual Orozco, a storekeeper, and Pancho Villa (whose real name was Doroteo Arango), a fugitive turned patriot. They raised an army, Madero joined them, and Revolution with a capital "R" broke out.

Finally accepting the inevitable, Diaz hurried into voluntary exile on May 24, 1911. Two weeks later Madero victoriously entered Mexico City and became president. Less than two years after, Madero was executed by reactionary forces. Five more years of internal strife followed, during which the United States intervened shamefully, doing little to cement good relationships between the two countries.

On February 5, 1917, a new constitution was adopted, which confirmed the one promulgated on the same date in 1857 by Juarez but which added important changes. In November of 1920 Alvaro Obregon was elected president. Modern Mexico dates from the time that Obregon took initial steps toward carrying out the social program of the Revolution as set forth in the Constitution of 1917.

VICIOUS FIGHTING took place in the mountains, on the plains, in city streets. Although the struggle ostensibly pitted rebels against government forces, freedom against despotism, ideals were frequently confused in the heat of confrontation and men often died at the hands of their partisans. Scenes above are of sharpshooters firing down on advancing troops and, in silhouette, making perfect targets of themselves. Below: during street fighting in Juarez, man at right has reloaded and calmly waits his turn to fire around corner of building.

Mexico West
Sun and Sea and Sand

CALIFORNIA AND ARIZONA nudge a generous portion of next-door Mexico. Though a boundary divides the two countries that call themselves United States (Mexicans pointedly refer to us as "north americans"), a continuity of cultures gives to our southwest such colorful town names as Ajo (garlic), and to Mexican settlements such anglicized designations as Benjamin Hill. Except for a brief pause at the border's entry point, a traveler would hardly be aware of just when he had left the U.S. and entered the Republic of Mexico.

If a traveler wanted more than a first taste of Mexico and penetrated deeply into its western gateway, he would discover a thousand miles of empty, sun-drenched beaches fronting the Sea of Cortez and the Pacific Ocean. He could also encounter all the comforts of home.

Mexico really has two western edges. One is pure Mexican, a composite of local women scrubbing clothes along a stream, fishermen selling their catch at morning light, and Indians weaving coarse fabrics on primitively efficient belt looms. The other is a sometimes jangling mixture of swinging nightclubs, elegant hotels, and posh restaurants peopled more by denizens of Los Angeles than of Ciudad Mexico.

From Puerto Penasco to Puerto Vallarta, most visions of "the real Mexico" are reflected along the country's western edge. In the south, at least, burros still clop over the cobblestones, but as often as not they are edged to the side by campers and Cadillacs. The brilliance of bougainvillea and jacaranda still emblazons crumbling walls, but their colors are sometimes outshown by the hues of serapes machine-made for the tourist trade. Though some of its patina is wearing a bit thin, Mexico's west remains one of the republic's most picturesque regions, one of its most colorful provincial areas.

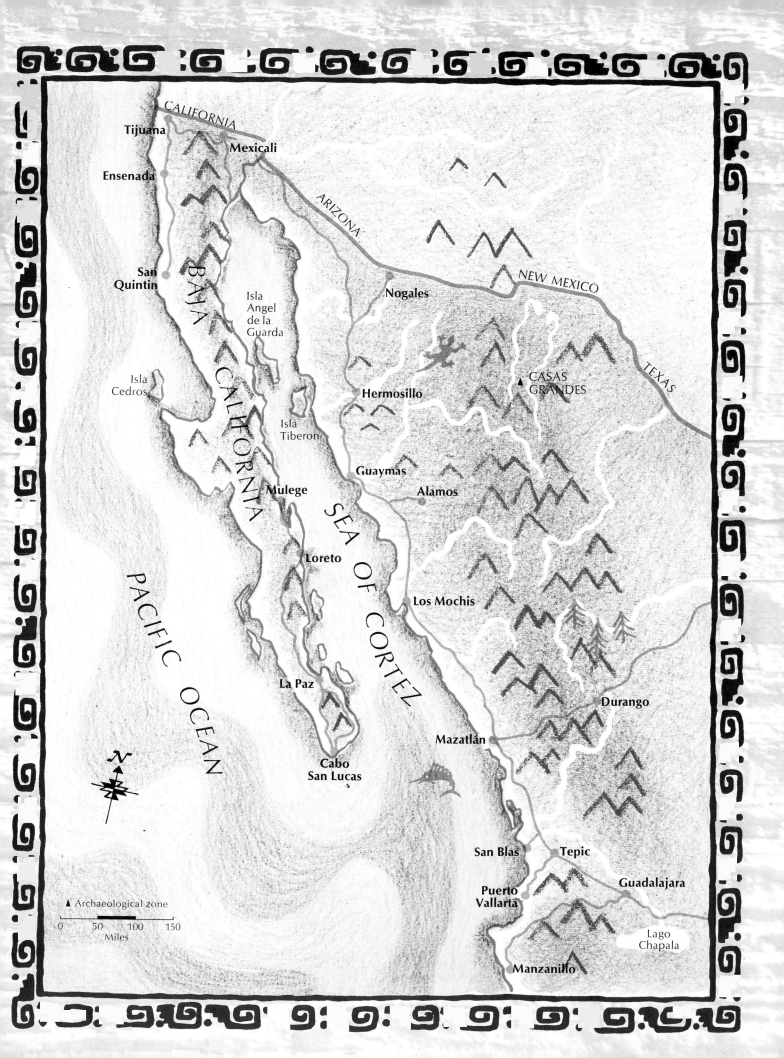

BAJA CALIFORNIA
True Wilderness...Plush Frontier

Paved roads from the border strike out bravely down the peninsula, only to fade into faint tracks heading forlornly across the wasteland. Forest-clad high sierra changes abruptly to flinty desert. Vast tracts of primitive wilderness butt up against isolated hotels accessible only by air or sea. Baja California is a huge natural history preserve, an untamed world pocked incongruously with resort areas guaranteed to satisfy the most sybaritic.

NO PLACE IN BAJA is far from the sea. Three ferries churn across the Sea of Cortez from mainland ports of Mazatlan, Topolobampo, Guaymas, carrying passengers and autos to La Paz, capital of Baja, opposite. Anchored off Mulege, left, a shrimp boat drowses in a golden world, accompanied by several patient pelicans. Landbound only for the night, a fisherman, above, mends net with timeworn gnarled hands.

THREE THOUSAND MILES of beach, most of it isolated and uninhabited, rim the peninsula. Hotels and luxury resorts are concentrated on the east coast, especially at San Jose del Cabo (above), La Paz, Loreto, Mulege. Weather is more kindly there than on the sometimes fog-bound Pacific side. Inland Baja has dry deserts or rugged mountains, infrequent villages, few paved roads.

TRANQUILITY PREVAILS, both in place and name, whether at La Palmilla, left, or at La Paz, below. Like the land, the people of Baja are as yet little touched by commercialism, unhurried, and carefree. Though the Mexican government has far-reaching plans for tourist development, lack of fresh water is a serious deterrent.

FISHING FLEET bobs at anchor in the coolness of morning while sportsmen and supplies are taken out to the boats by skiff. Happy fisherman opposite unloads a modest-sized catch.

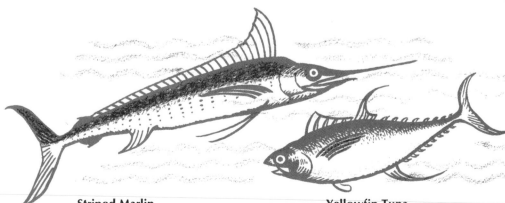

Striped Marlin
Also called *agujon, pez puereo*. Weight to 425 pounds.

Yellowfin Tuna
Commonly known as albacore. Weight to 450 pounds.

SEA OF CORTEZ
No Other Place where Game Fish are so Abundant

On maps it is called matter-of-factly the Gulf of California. But to anyone who *knows*, it is the Sea of Cortez. In this western inland ocean, lying between Baja California and the Mexican mainland, the varieties of marine life are encyclopedic. Its shores are idyllic. Its islands, never out of sight from either coast, are an experience for the explorer, the diver, the fisherman.

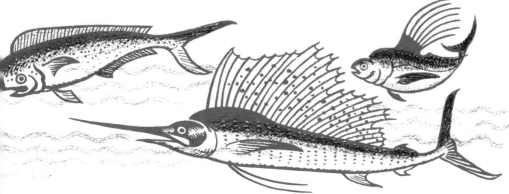

Dolphinfish
Also called *dorado*, *mahimahi*. Weight to 80 pounds.

Pacific Sailfish
Called spearfish, *pez vela*. Weight to 295 pounds.

Roosterfish
Called *pez gallo*. Weight to 35 pounds.

FIVE FIGHTING FISH OF THE CORTEZ
There are fish, and there are fish. The variety of finned game in this inland sea is enormous, but those depicted here are some of the finest. The Sea of Cortez has been called a living broth of sea life.

The Seris: Nomadic Turtle Hunters of the Upper Gulf

 Desemboque, Puerto de la Libertad, and Tiburon Island all lie on the Sea of Cortez, in the dry northwestern corner of Sonora. Undistinguished settlements that are seldom seen by the casual visitor, they are nevertheless home for one of Mexico's most independent and primitive people—the Seri Indians.

Numbering fewer than 300, and located only in this region of the republic, the Seris are a freedom loving group that has refused to be integrated into society, in spite of repeated efforts by the Mexican government. They have never been Christianized, because of deep-rooted resentment against the Spaniards, preferring to worship the god of the sea and the god of the earth, represented as a mole.

Semi-nomadic, they occasionally head into the desert to gather cactus fruit, but for the most part they dwell near the water, living off the wealth of the sea. Despite their isolation, a small band at Kino Bay has become somewhat of a tourist attraction, selling fine wood carvings and posing grudgingly for pictures—for a few pesos.

SERI HANDICRAFTS speak of the sea and a life close to nature. Delicate necklaces at right have paper-thin shells with tiny black seed shells in their centers or veined olive shells strung with fish vertebrae. The carved and polished ironwood turtles are prized even among the Indians. Visitors to a Seri settlement, opposite, find the inhabitants standoffish but willing and tough bargainers.

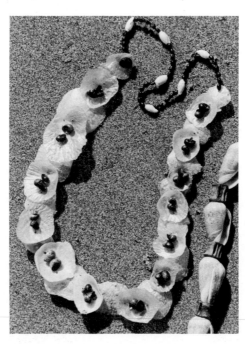

TURTLE COOKOUT, done simply by building a fire on top of the dead creature, is best observed well upwind. Reputed to have once been cannibals, the taciturn Seris now subsist chiefly on sea life.

Northwestern Mexico does not have grand cathedrals and churches like those built across the central plateau in colonial times. To the Spanish, the land in the north was harsh, scarcely worth settling, and they left its opening to the hard-working friars and padres. Today, touring the missions founded by Father Eusebio Francisco Kino in the late 1600's is a most pleasant side trip on the way to Hermosillo or Guaymas from Nogales. Many of the structures are in ruins, but off Highways 2 and 15 churches are still in use at Caborca, Pitiquito, Oquitoa, Adid, and Tubatama.

KINO MISSIONS

Northernmost Traces of Imperial Spain

TUBATAMA AND CABORCA, above and right, both mark mission sites that were destroyed during the bloody Pima rebellion in 1695. These missions had major rank among those established by Padre Kino. Caborca is built on a scale similar to that of San Xavier in Arizona.

RUINS OF COCOSPERA mission church, opposite, stand on a prominent hill between Imuris and Cananea. Present building, constructed in 18th century around original adobe church built by Padre Kino, was raided often by Apaches, used as a fortress by Mexican, American, and French adventurers.

Driving deep into Mexico is...different

Like the United States, Mexico has fine highways and well maintained thoroughfares. But below the border there is a vast difference in how those roads are used. Though not careless or reckless, Mexican drivers have their own law of logic, their unique code of ethics, and it behooves a driver new to the country to have a healthy respect for these, even though he does not understand them.

SLEEPING POLICEMEN is nickname given to topes, above, which are designed to slow traffic through a spine-jarring shock. Local drivers sometimes surreptitiously remove certain knobs, enabling them to safely whiz through the obstacle at high speed. At right, road construction or damaged highway is often barricaded with a row of rocks, a pile of foliage, or whatever else comes to hand.

DISABLED BUSES are a common sight
(top of page). Such breakdowns are
taken philosophically for what they
are: an opportunity to picnic or rest in
the shade. More of a hazard are
domestic animals, ranging in mass from
dogs to cows, that claim territorial
rights to all roads.

ALAMOS
A Town Where Time has Little Meaning

One of the very few places unspoiled by discovery, creaky old Alamos continues to show little outward change even after years of being a favored destination for visitors driving beyond Guaymas and Ciudad Obregon on Highway 15. Laws protect the former mining town against undue "progress" by keeping billboards, neon signs, and gas stations out of the central part of town and by restricting architecture to Spanish colonial style.

PLAZA DE ARMAS, deserted and silent in the noonday heat, comes briefly to life when afternoon shadows lengthen and the still air begins to cool. The town's quiet character and unhurried pace attract U.S. citizens, who have remodeled some of the handsome old homes and retired in Alamos to live the good life far from newspapers and television.

LANDMARK CHURCH, La Senora de La Concepcion, dates back to the late 18th century. Behind church, but not visible in picture above, is a low building which once housed a Japanese silk factory. The lovely arched arcades facing Alamos plaza, left, are a cool retreat when the sun is high. On the west side of the plaza is Hotel Los Portales, housed in a former mansion.

...Alamos

ARCHES, COLONNADES, COURTYARDS are remnants of Spanish colonialism in Alamos, where time breathes visibly, but gently. Once a brawling mining center, Alamos is now but a gentle whisper of its past, a place no longer wealthy in minerals but rich in a peace and quiet that is beyond monetary value.

MONUMENTAL PROGRAM at the tiny Alamos Theater lures a young romantic for a moment of wistful diversion from more worldly matters. Price of shoeshine, in pre-inflation centavos, amounts to about five cents American. Because of its mining past, Alamos is a storehouse of legends concerning lost mines, buried treasures, and fabulous extravagances. One industrious silver baron was supposed to have laid a path of silver bars between his mansion and the church for the passage of wedding guests. The principal industry today —and certainly its liveliest one—is the gathering of the jumping bean.

Village life is the same today as it has been for a thousand yesterdays

A comfortable familiarity reaches out as one travels from one small Mexican town to another. They are so much alike that you could almost be moved blindfolded and find each village plan the same. The result is a warm sense of having been there before that makes even a foreigner feel at home.

GENERAL STORE (tienda) is one of the busiest places on a town's main plaza after siesta time, when women and children scurry in and out in preparation for the evening meal. In earlier, slower-moving hours of the day, the local store may become a gathering place for the "cracker barrel" set, much as it was in the United States two generations ago. CONASUPO refers to a government price control program instrumental in the purchasing and marketing of basic necessities. The village pictured here and opposite is Ures, in northern Sonora, formerly capital of the state.

ROMANTIC STATUARY, bandstand, and trees are all basic to the Mexican plaza. The larger the town, the more grand the plaza may be. Usually the most prominent landmark is the church, below, a hub for the most important events in a Mexican's life: baptism, confirmation, first communion, marriage, death.

Church

Market-place

Stores and shops

Government palace

A CHURCH, A BANDSTAND . . . MEXICO'S BASIC TOWN PLAN
Main plaza, virtually identical in almost every village or town in Mexico, is the spot around which stand the church and local government offices, traditionally the first structures in the founding of a settlement.

GUAYMAS/MAZATLAN
Northern Meccas for Southern California Sportsmen

Linked by 400 miles of Nogales-Mexico City coastal Highway 15, Guaymas and Mazatlan have much in common, despite the distance between. Both are the proverbial fisherman's paradise; both teem with marsh and inland wildlife ranging from doves to ducks to deer. Both have beautiful bays and beaches. Protected by the Sea of Cortez, Guaymas is more sheltered and warmer year round. Mazatlan, being open to the Pacific, has more surf and is occasionally hit by ocean-going storms.

NETS AND RUGS create splashes of riotous color on the waterfront. Though Guaymas, left, is some 400 miles north of Mazatlan, above, they are linked by the common lifeblood of the ocean. Having been an active commercial fishing port for many years, Guaymas is creaking and weather worn and has the ripe aroma of the sea. Mazatlan, more open to Pacific breezes and perhaps more of a tourist center, has a harbor dotted with islands, which are favored picnic and swimming places.

SAN CARLOS BAY, below, is a lovely resort area just north of Guaymas. It and nearby Bocochibampo Bay offer all manner of water sports and social life at a variety of fine hotels at the water's edge. Mazatlan's great promenade, opposite, curves around the bay fronting the town, is a gathering place for residents in early evening to watch the spectacular sunset. Horse-drawn carriages called aranas (spiders) rattle through the city streets and are a fine way to tour the town.

Four Days of Fun and Fish

Guaymas was the place where the first Sea of Cortez billfish was caught with rod and reel. So for the past 25 years, citizens have found it appropriate to annually fling a four-day fishing tournament known as the Fiesta de la Pesca. Hundreds of sportsmen from the north hurry down to Guaymas to vie for the Governor's "Biggest Fish" trophy or the award for the most tags and releases. The bash is heralded by a noisy opening parade of horn-hooting boats in the harbor and climaxed by a wild closing fiesta in one of the town's largest dining halls.

Fish do not run according to timetables, so the fiesta may be held any time from May to July. Write the Guaymas Chamber of Commerce for details.

Mazatlan is the center for one of Mexico's biggest pre-Lenten celebrations. At the end of February or beginning of March, a giant carnival explodes, complete with Roman candles and rockets, masks, and mariachi bands. Tourists are fair game for cranium-crowning with *cascarones* (dyed eggshells filled with multicolored bits of paper) but catch their breath at the traditional burning of an effigy called "Bad Humor." For additional entertainment, there are three parades in three days and at least two grand balls, not to mention a bullfight and other festivities.

Most guide books list Mazatlan hotels but give no hint of the room shortage at carnival time. Reservations should be made several months in advance before all space is sold.

DETOUR TO DURANGO
Side Trip into Western High Country

Less than ten miles south of Mazatlan, Highway 40 heads east, up into the rugged Sierra Madre Occidental. Three hundred miles beyond is Durango, capital of the state of the same name. This is the only road crossing the formidable mountain chain that stretches from Arizona to Guadalajara, traversing some of the most spectacular high country in all of Mexico.

MAGNIFICENT SCENERY unfolds
shortly after highway climbs east out of
Mazatlan. Well paved and maintained,
the road swoops and loops back on
itself, rising high into the Sierra Madre
Occidental, left. Roadway is often
crossed by deer in the evening; bear
are common at higher elevations but
are seldom seen. The final visual
reward is Durango's cathedral, above.

The Huichols: Corn and Peyote are Gods that Bless a Sacred People

HOLY WEEK PROCESSION circles solemnly around the church, led by the "governor" and shamans carrying their branches of power. Holy Week, the corn festivities, and the peyote trial are important ceremonies in this ritualistic society.

The rugged mountains of the Sierra de Nayarit north of Guadalajara are the homeland of the Huichol Indians. These were among the last tribes to come under Spanish rule, and their religion still is essentially pagan, centering around agricultural deities. The deer is a sacred animal, its blood a symbol of fertility. Corn is the source of all life. Peyote is the means of communication with the gods. The unity of these three elements is the absolute core of Huichol beliefs. They are gods.

In the corn ceremonies, the Huichols remember the origins of woman, for it was Nacahue, mother of all gods, who gave the tender part of the corn to the first man for planting, and from it was born the first Huichol woman.

The peyote trial is a deeply religious experience. Those who make a pilgrimage in search of the plant—which grows in the birthplace of the gods—are holy ones who seek to rise beyond their mortal state and communicate with the deities.

TATATA NUITZICAME is the Christ of the Huichol Indians. During Holy Week, the wooden body of Christ, above, is adorned with sacred feathers and swathed in fabric. Then it is placed on a bed of leaves on the floor while men and women, led by the native priest, sing and chant, left. Feathers are the means through which communication is established with the sun god, since it is believed that the eagle ascends the closest to Heaven.

SHAMAN invokes blessing of the gods, utilizing gestures and items used in other Huichol religious ceremonies. Feathers in his hat are symbols of status as a maarakame, or native priest. Belt has woven into it design of the tutu flower, symbol of corn, which along with peyote and the deer form a sacred Huichol trinity.

BASKETS OF PEYOTE are reverently sorted, left, after a 600-mile pilgrimage to Virikuta, legendary place of the gods. The holy plant is shared in a ritual that brings special favor to those who partake of it. In ceremony below, a man readies a candle before carrying it to sacred mountain where the sun was born. Yarn painting, a beautiful Huichol craft, has its roots in their pagan religion.

SAN BLAS/PUERTO VALLARTA
Everyone Goes to Get Away from it All

Draw a straight line west from Guadalajara
and it will hit the Pacific Coast at Puerto
Vallarta. Bend the line due north, to San Blas.
Once a quiet fishing settlement, Puerto Vallarta became
an "in" place during the 1960's; it now has resort hotels
and all the other trappings of a seashore resort. San Blas
is yet a rustic village, long since discovered but still
peaceful and picturesque, a destination for travelers who
shun the luxuries of Mexico's more tourist-oriented towns.

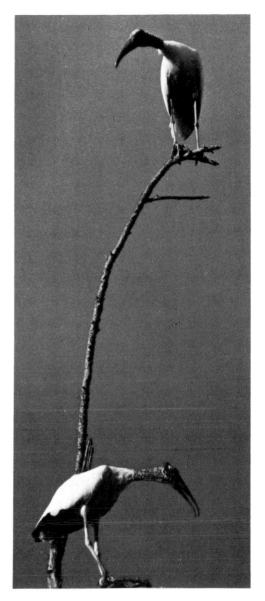

SAN BLAS, shown on this page and opposite, is the proverbial tropical paradise, a dreamer's vision of the South Seas. The pace of life is languid, the people gentle and open. Early morning, when fish nets are hauled in, brings flocks of ocean-going gulls and pelicans. The nearby jungle abounds in wading birds; left to right: snake bird, white heron, wood ibis.

PUERTO VALLARTA *is people. Once a place to get away from it all, it is no longer the escapist's dream it was before the film "Night of the Iguana" thrust it into the public eye and started a tourist rush from the U.S. Los Muertos, above and opposite, the favorite beach, is equipped with beachboys, boats, and broiled fish. Puerto Vallarta's least-kept secret is a boat trip down the coast to Yelapa, a delightful village with grass huts and chiggers.*

Tequila: never less than three nor more than thirty-three

A drink of distinction, Tequila has brought world renown to a small Mexican village. Though many other beverages are made from the familiar "century plant," only that from Tequila, state of Jalisco, can rightfully be called by that name. To Tequila, a timeworn toast: "Never less than three, nor more than thirty-three."

GIGANTIC PINEAPPLES, as the hearts of the maguey plants are called, are loaded into steam ovens, above, then shredded and the juice pressed out to ferment in large vats, right. Two distillations produce the fiery liquor known all over Mexico as tequila.

PORTION OF À MURAL in the Sauza plant, town of Tequila, reveals happy goings-on. One authority comments, "I don't know if this sort of thing went on in the factories all the time, or whether this was only an annual fiesta."

HARVEST TIME in the fields means hacking the spiky leaves off the maguey plant, left, an honored trade. Above, barrels of tequila are loaded aboard a truck to be taken away for aging. Though tequila is ready to drink in less than a week after harvest, the connoisseur's choice ages in wooden casks for periods of several months to as much as seven years. Aging process changes the clear liquid to a golden color, hallmark of a fine tequila.

PLAZA DE LA LIBERACION stretches grandly from the back of the cathedral, above, to Degollado Theater (see page 68), is one of Mexico's most handsome plazas. Guadalajara's cathedral is distinguished by its wild lack of architectural unity, being a hodgepodge of Corinthian, Byzantine, Doric, and several other styles. Nevertheless, it is a grand landmark and a source of local pride, and its form is used as a symbol of the city.

GUADALAJARA

Fountains, Flowers, and Orozco on the Ceiling

 Second largest city in Mexico, Guadalajara is just four airplane hours from Los Angeles, two driving days below the Arizona border. Booming but not bustling, modern but not metropolitan, the city of flowers and fountains preserves an ambient air unlike any other place in Mexico. Parks, plazas, mariachi bands, and cockfights make Guadalajara a place in which to spend weeks rather than days.

BREATHTAKING BEAUTY of murals by native son Jose Clemente Orozco covers the stone walls and ceilings of the chapel of Hospicio Cabanas, an orphanage also blessed with flower filled patios and laughing children. Benches in the chapel are provided for lying-down viewing of the dome's famed "Man of Fire." One of Orozco's most compelling murals, an earlier work depicting Hidalgo leading the struggle against Spain, is above the stairway in the Governor's Palace (see page 22).

GRACEFUL GINGERBREAD
bandstand in Plaza de Armas,
right, alongside the cathedral, is a
popular gathering place on weekend
evenings. Gracious old Degollado
Theater, below, features outstanding
concert and drama performances.
Opposite, one of the city's many
fountains sparkles and splashes near an
open-air cafe.

Craft Towns of Guadalajara

In and around Guadalajara are so many craftsmen at work that the area is a recognized popular arts center on a par with Oaxaca and Michoacan. Guadalajara is noted for its colored blown glass, leather handbags and clothing, gold and silver jewelry, candles, lamps, tin mirror frames, candelabra, and plaster religious figures.

Casa de las Artesanias, at the north end of Parque Agua Azul, is a state-operated institution for displaying and selling handicrafts of the state of Jalisco.

Several nearby towns are noted for various craft specialties:

Zapopan. Huichol Indian yarn "paintings," colorful yarn God's eyes, woven shoulder bags, rings, brace-lets. (These items are made in remote villages but are sold at the Basilica of Zapopan.)

Tlaquepaque. Molded ceramic figures and caricature fruits, wooden furniture, textiles, glassware, pottery.

Tonala. Painted ceramics of many types—toys, piggy banks, masks, animals, flowers—papier mache animals, boxes, costume jewelry.

Santa Cruz. Crude ceramic piggy banks, clay whistles, and surrealistic figures.

El Rosario. Clay toys, pottery, water bottles, jars, tubs.

Jocotepec. Woven serapes with bold geometric designs and small flowers in pastel colors.

Ajijic. Woven fabrics, skirts, blouses, tablecloths, straw mats.

The bigger the band, the louder they play

Mexico's version of the wandering minstrels, mariachi bands are on hand for almost any kind of festive gathering. Their name supposedly comes from the French word for marriage, because during Maximilian's time they were often used for weddings. The state of Jalisco is home of the mariachis, but they are seen — and heard — everywhere south of the border.

THE MUSIC IS GOOD and it is loud in Guadalajara's Mariachi Plaza. On busy Sunday afternoons as many as five bands may be playing different tunes at the same time, each straining to outdo the others, all producing a grand cacophony of sound. So that their patrons may derive full benefit of their efforts, band members cluster around a table, their horns only a few eardrum-shattering feet away.

SPECIAL OCCASION brings out gorgeous tight pants, glittering buttons, gleaming teeth. Bands are hired for birthday parties and other celebrations, even for serenading a swain's only true love at ungodly hours of the night. Good bands have a wide repertory of songs, some full of passionate love, others whose lyrics are wildly hilarious. The number every musician is sick to death of, but which is requested mostly by North Americans, is "Guadalajara."

MANZANILLO
A Bay for Beachcombing, a Beach for Siesta

Below Guadalajara, on a stretch of south-looking coast, lies Manzanillo. Hardly undiscovered, but not yet a prime tourist attraction, Manzanillo is nevertheless an easy escape town. The best season is December through March; the rest of the year is rainy or hot and muggy. East and west of town are delicious portions of shoreline where the Pacific tumbles eternally over shifting sandbars into palm-ringed lagoons.

EMPTY BEACHES are still to be found on the tropical peninsula of Manzanillo, between Acapulco and Puerto Vallarta. However, far-reaching plans are being implemented to facelift the natural terrain, construct hotels and an international airport, and transform the area into a playground. Manzanillo harbor is a busy commercial seaport; in town are several shops that rent or sell fishing and diving equipment.

Less than one hour's drive from Guadalajara is famed Lake Chapala, Mexico's largest inland body of water. Light on night activities, the place comes to life on weekends when it jumps with local picnickers and Guadalajara families on holiday. Chapala offers boats and horses to hire, a country club, fine restaurants, hotels, art centers, and residential areas with a permanent international community that is well-stocked with North Americans.

LAKE CHAPALA
Sparkling Sunday Outings in an International Community

WATER HYACINTH chokes up far ends of lake, compelling fishermen to chop a channel for their boats, opposite. Water's edge in Chapala town, left, has a promenade, restaurants, a boisterous beer garden. Surrounded by low-lying mountains, the valley's ideal climate attracts American retirees to towns with such tongue tripping names as Ajijic, Ocotlan, Jocotepec, Cojijitlan (above).

South and West

A World of

AT DAYBREAK the dugouts glide away from the shores of Lake Patzcuaro to converge in tight circles on the mirrored surface. Long-handled nets, dipped deep into the water, are raised in unison like a salute to the gods of the waters, and a few fish flop into the canoes. By early morning the serious fishermen are breakfasting on a plate of watery frijoles and a cup of thin chocolate, relinquishing the lake to the heavily photographed dugouts that appear on cue when the first tourist-laden ferry arrives at Janitzio Island.

By mid-morning the day is already old for Toluca's turpentine gatherers, who make their rounds of tall pines with trunks scarred by deep V-shaped notches. They empty cups of fragrant resin into buckets, then hunker down to soften a few tortillas over a crackling fire.

By late morning all of the sidewalk cafes facing Morelia's main plaza are full. A Frenchman wanders by, searching for a place to sit. Two Mexicans move their coffee cups aside and invite the *turisto* to share their table, extending the invitation with gallant gestures. Settling back, they watch in friendly curiosity to see what the stranger will order for breakfast.

At noon a lady from Texas asks the driver of the Acapulco-bound bus when he expects to stop for lunch. After the third plaintive request he pulls the vehicle off the road at Mezcala so his passenger can buy a Coke. Three children rush up, thrusting foot-long iguanas at the *norteamericana*. She retreats to the back of the bus, her eyes glazed, her hunger forgotten.

By ten in the evening, Acapulco's night people have siesta'd, showered their sunburned skins, and dressed in shirts and skirts that are reminiscent of Hawaii. While sipping *colo-locos* they try to decide whether to dine Polynesian, or Continental, or Mexican buffet.

of the Capital
Natural Beauty

Morelia

Toluca Mexico City

Lago Patzcuaro Nevado de Toluca Cuernavaca

Patzcuaro

Uruapan

Taxco

Oaxaca

MONTE ALBAN ▲ ▲ MITLA

El Infiernillo

Playa Azul Zihuatanejo Acapulco Puerto Escondido

PACIFIC OCEAN

N

▲ Archaeological zone

0   50   100   150
Miles

MICHOACAN
Everything that is Natural and Beautiful

Its mist-shrouded valleys, its alpine peaks, and its sparkling lakes have given Michoacan the name of "Little Switzerland." But it is also strongly reminiscent of old Japan, because of the beautiful creations in wood by the Tarascans, who have learned to live in harmony with their environment. Whatever you call it, Michoacan possesses a rare appeal that transcends time and place, moving one a little closer to nature.

AS IN A JAPANESE PAINTING, the Tarascan village of Angahuan huddles low in early morning mists, opposite. Horses can be hired here for a bone-joggling ride through volcanic ash and barren lava beds to the foot of Paricutin volcano, which erupted in violent birth in 1943. Terraced fountain, above, is in lush Ruiz National Park at Uruapan—a wonderland of cascades, falls, and rapids. It is fed by the Cupatitzio River, which hurries along south of town to thunder in a magnificent 100-foot drop at Tzararacua Falls, left.

Popular arts come directly from the hands of the people

Unlike some of the commonplace items ground out by machine and peddled in large quantities all over the country, the arts of Michoacan come honestly and directly from the hands of the people. Fashioned with care in the manner that has been traditional for centuries, they are evidence of a joy in creating.

BASKETWORK is a popular as well as practical craft practiced all over Mexico by hand-weaving long, plaited reeds. At left, a Tarascan uses a wooden plug as a form to insure symmetrical shape and a tight weave. The town of Paracho, in Michoacan, is known as the guitar town because almost every resident from youngster up through grandfather is busily engaged in some stage of creating them. Above, a craftsman carefully pares wood away from the neck, after which he will attach frets, then string the instrument.

TINY TARASCAN girl, left, weaves bright sashes, using a belt loom. She shyly offers them for sale alongside the road. Though seen in many parts of the country, the colorful, dyed fiber chair seats, lacquer trays, ceramic bird, and papier mache figure represent some of the fine handcrafted specialties of the area west of Mexico City.

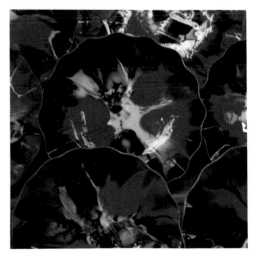

Profile of Mexico
PATZCUARO
Colonial Capital of the Land of Hummingbirds

The tiny hummingbird was important in the
folklore of the old Tarascans, and the
ancients used its scintillating feathers in their
folk art. Still reminiscent of the vivid colors and vitality
of the lovely birds are the town and lake of Patzcuaro,
both exquisitely of another century
in atmosphere and appearance.

GRAND INDIAN MARKET, opposite, is held on Friday, when Tarascans swarm to town by canoe, burro, or on foot. As if one charming plaza weren't enough, Patzcuaro has two. Plaza Grande, this page, is a block away from Plaza Chica; both are surrounded by low, tile-roofed buildings and cobbled streets. For a special treat, drive or walk west on Calle Ponce de Leon, at north end of Plaza Grande. It climbs up a narrow cobblestone way that is closed in on both sides by stately cedars, and finally reaches the top of El Estribo (the stirrup), one of Mexico's loveliest spots, with a panoramic view of all of Lake Patzcuaro, its villages and islands.

SOLEMN DEATH WATCH, opposite, is held in the cemetery on Lake Patzcuaro's Janitzio Island on November 2. Villagers decorate graves with flowers and spread a repast for the dead, then sit a candlelit vigil until daybreak, waiting for the departed souls to partake of the food.

EARLY MORNING brings net fishermen out on calm Lake Patzcuaro. Several dugout canoes are formed into a circle, and large butterfly-shaped nets are slipped into the water on the ends of long poles. Everyone levers up his net toward the center at the same time, trapping any fish that may be there. Since the catch is usually small, fishermen gladly pose for pictures in return for several pesos.

CALZADA DE GUADALUPE, right, knows only the murmur of soft conversation for most of the year, except on December 12, when the stone causeway is the scene of a religious procession to the Sanctuary of Guadalupe, a gold-leaf gingerbread church at its eastern limit. At the other end of the street, toward downtown area, its extension passes under the grand arches of a stone aqueduct that was constructed in the late 1700's. Nearby is the small Callejon de Romance (Lovers' Lane), where bright bougainvillea spills over walls inset with tile plaques bearing quotations by the romantic Michoacan poet Lucas Ortiz. The lane has two fountains where housewives gather to gossip and children splash each other with water and screams of delight.

Profile of Mexico
MORELIA
Quiet Corner of Old-World Charm

Halfway between Mexico City and Guadalajara is Morelia, capital of Michoacan state, colonial center, courtly city. It is also a surprise municipality because few visitors are aware of its existence, even though it has a population of 150,000. Morelia is the kind of place that offers not fun and excitement but charm, calm, and contentment all in ample measure.

SAN FRANCISCO CHURCH, above, dates back to 1541, only twenty years after the Spanish conquest. Its courtyard is a peaceful retreat for students and visitors needing a change from the bustle around the main plaza. Morelia Cathedral, left, faces a long line of restaurant arcades. More than 100 years in the building, the cathedral is constructed of delicate pink stone, except for its sparkling, tiled cupolas.

BLAST OF TRUMPETS, boom of drums, wail of voices are heard daily throughout the land as impromptu groups of musicians give out with their best. Talent isn't a prerequisite; spirit and staying power mean the most.

Music makers add many a happy note to a melodious life

Evidence notwithstanding, not everyone in Mexico is a born musician. Mexico's music may have its roots in Spain and its fiber in natural Indian rhythms, but most of it springs spontaneously from pure inventive genius, from the instinct to live by letting life flow out and all around.

GRAND STREET BAND, featuring a sizeable brass section, plays lustily for some local event, the importance of which is often lost in the joy of the music. Bandstands such as that at left are the scene of weekend concerts in most Mexican towns.

TERRIFYING TRACK UP NEVADO DE TOLUCA, an extinct volcano, cuts across the face of precipitous slopes covered with huge chunks of black lava, above timber line. The roadway, barely wide enough for a small car in most places, climbs to almost 15,000 feet, then drops over the crater's rim to the mysterious Lakes of the Sun and the Moon. At these altitudes, chill creeps quickly into the bones, and the only sound is the sighing of the wind. The trip is not recommended for the faint or weak of heart, or for an undependable car.

TOLUCA
Death's Heads...and Driving into a Volcano

From time immemorial the city of Toluca has been touted for its grand municipal market. Huge though it is, there are more interesting markets in Guadalajara and Guanajuato, more variety in Oaxaca and Patzcuaro. But this doesn't detract from Toluca's glory, the best of which is not to be found in town but in the surrounding countryside.

MOUNTAIN RANCH, left, lies in lush, green foothills of the Nevado, where the air is crisp yet warm and where cheerful wildflowers cover the slopes in springtime. Macabre figures above are typical of the death's-head sculpture of Metepec, a village just out of Toluca, where stucco house fronts are painted in hot, joyous colors.

TAXCO
Tourist Town Built by Silver

Once regarded as Mexico's most picturesque hideaway, Taxco is no longer the storybook village of years gone by but more of a shopping stopover for travelers headed from Mexico City to Acapulco. Yet beyond the dining room decor and behind the well-stocked souvenir shops, there is still a Taxco that warrants exploration. On the circuitous side streets that meander up the steep hillsides, much of the old mood prevails.

SPARKLING ARRAY of silver work dazzles the eye and tempts the pocketbook in Taxco's stores and talleres (workshops). Though the town's fame rests chiefly on its silver, as corroborated by tourists who make brief stops for shopping, Taxco exudes charm that is best discovered by exploring the steep streets and back alleyways where the casual visitor seldom ventures.

TINY CENTRAL PLAZA fronts a famed landmark, the parochial church of Santa Prisca, whose gorgeous Baroque construction was financed in the mid-1700's by Jose de la Borda, a Frenchman who came into silver bonanza in the area. Borda's creed was said to be "God gives to Borda, so Borda gives to God." And give to God he did, by way of elaborate constructions in Taxco, Cuernavaca, and Mexico City. Taxco's fame as a popular silver crafts center was brought about by William Spratling, an energetic American who in the early 1900's revived the town's dying arts.

CUERNAVACA
Garden Spot Stopover on the Southern Health Spa Route

EXOTIC BIRDS SHARE LAWNS and gardens of charming Hotel Las Mananitas, below, in Cuernavaca, historically a retreat for Aztecs, Spaniards, Frenchmen, Mexicans, and North Americans. The city is also known for its Borda Gardens, the Palace of Cortes, and a colonial cathedral, whose interior has been starkly and beautifully simplified. In the incongruous scene opposite, a yoga class duplicates the pose struck by a modern sculpture at Ixtapan de la Sal, a resort hotel with Mexican-Disneyland decor, and one of the many spas between Mexico City and Acapulco.

Long a retreat for vacationers from the United States and a goal for retirees anxious to live the good life below the border, Cuernavaca is also a popular stop-off on the way to the coast from Mexico City. Even if the glory of the Borda Gardens is not quite all it used to be, and although Cortes' palace seems to be undergoing eternal remodeling, ample diversions make quiet Cuernavaca a most pleasant change from the frenetic capital.

Flowers create an open-air greenhouse

Bougainvillea

Prickly poppy

Flame vine

Ageratum

Flowers are inspiration for the brilliant hues that the Mexican uses in his arts and crafts. He sells bouquets door to door, on street corners, and in the middle of busy traffic intersections. Flower motifs decorate his folk art; fresh flowers are standard decor in many Mexican hotel rooms; throughout most of the year the Mexican countryside glows with blooms. The Mexican considers flowers as much a part of his life as food or music. To say that he loves flowers is like saying that Latin blood runs in his veins.

Butterfly weed

Wild cotton

Indian paint brush

Coral tree

ACAPULCO
The Resort that has Everything Under the Sun

Acapulco often is the beginning and end of Mexico for the hyperactive visitor who jets in, forces himself to idle away a few days, then whisks out again. Though Acapulco is no more representative of Mexico than Coney Island is typical of the United States, its air of leisure is quite contagious. Loafing is tolerated, but sleeping is barely acceptable, and then only after hours of night life.

BEACHES, HOTELS, and people on, in, and between is an apt description of Acapulco. Across the bay, right, stretches Playa Hornos, locally referred to as afternoon beach because conditions are supposed to be best there for sunning and funning after 1 P.M. To the west (left, out of picture) is Playa Caleta, "morning beach," with its off-lying island of Roqueta, famed for beer-drinking burros and clear diving waters. Playa Condesa, opposite page, fronts some of Acapulco's most impressively plush waterside hotels.

TIME OF LEISURE is enjoyed at brunch on the bay, left, or soccer on the sand, below. Sailing, skin diving, water skiing, and sunset watching are but a few of the diversions of this Mexican resort of resorts.

"...and the Time to Enjoy..."

Salud y pesetas, y tiempo para gastarlas, goes a popular toast in Mexico: Health and money, and the time to enjoy them. It is a pledge that puts time in its proper place.

Whereas the North American tends to be a slave to watches and clocks, marking his life in minutes and hours, time is of only marginal value to the Mexican, who vaguely notes its passage in days or years.

Let time pass, enjoy it. It is for man's convenience. Time is something to be disposed of, not to be a slave to.

Literally, the word *manana* means tomorrow. Practically, it can denote a week or a month hence—especially if a promise or commitment is involved.

Another word that spices the tasty conversational ragout of Mexicans is *ahora.* Dictionaries define the word as "now," but it really means any point in time from the present to infinity. More imperative is *ahorita,* literally "in a jiffy." In practical matters, however, it signifies "before too long." *Momentito* is a little minute, measured urgently by a quarter-inch of space between thumb and forefinger. It means "sooner or later."

Time in Mexico is not an important ingredient in the banquet of life. It is a side dish enhancing the entrees—health and money.

*"A CROSS BETWEEN WAIKIKI,
Coney Island, and Tahiti, though
delightful in the morning hours,"
is how Acapulco has been described.
Late in May and again at the end of
December, government offices in
Mexico City shut down for two weeks
and employees vanish from the capital.
The most likely place to find affluent
officials then is Acapulco. Such
sybaritic scenes as those on this page
and opposite seem to belie the fact
that Guerrero, the state in which
Acapulco lies, is one of Mexico's most
primitive regions, with deep jungle
that has never been penetrated
by explorers.*

Profile of Mexico
COSTA BRAVA
In the West, Some Places are Yet to be Discovered

Above and below Acapulco is a smooth sweep of sand and sea, little-trod by the casual visitor but not unnoticed by the Mexican government, which has an eye on the tourist potential of this climate-blessed stretch of ocean front. Zihuatanejo may be well on its way to becoming a latter-day Acapulco, but the coast between is still full of surprises. And south of Acapulco, few tourists venture.

FROM ZIHUATANEJO, opposite, to Puerto Escondido, above, the waves wash gently on beaches of the Pacific Coast. Once this coast was a discovery spot—and some of its villages (such as Penotepa, left) still are relatively untouched by tourism. But improved communications and access are making the stretch of coast more popular. The government plans to develop the entire region and expects to build hotels at selected sites above and below Acapulco.

Mexico North
Still a Frontier Spirit

NORTHERN MEXICO has been called an anteroom to Old Mexico. It is a broad gateway for Texans who brave cheerless scenery and dry deserts to get to the more hospitable landscapes farther south.

Two principal routes start at the border and traverse portions of the north's alkali tablelands before climbing into the more appealing highlands of the great central plateau. Despite an initially monotonous regularity, both are heavily traveled by motorists heading deep into the republic.

The Central Highway begins at El Paso and the once-sinful Ciudad Juarez, and unrolls through desert and cattlelands. From Chihuahua on, green farmlands and irrigated fields relieve the weary landscape. The Pan American Highway—the most direct route for motorists starting from San Antonio—enters Mexico at Laredo and courses through rough mountain terrain, skirting mining centers that whisper of their former vigor. There may be faster routes, but this is one of the most scenic, especially below Tamazunchale (called Thomas-and-Charley), where the road climbs from 700 feet to 5000 feet in only 60 miles before heading into Otomi Indian country.

The closer the traveler gets to the capital, the more his eye is saturated with yards-high political slogans that somehow remain—even between election years. *"Arriba y adelante,"* they shout: Onward and upward.

And onward and upward the road goes. In the hills of Hidalgo country, head frames of old mines lean over shaft entrances that gape like empty eye sockets. Buildings are warped crazily, tin roofs rusted and sagging.

In Mexico's big plateau land, top-of-the-world vistas invite the traveler to linger and explore the southern mining empire of Guanajuato and Queretaro.

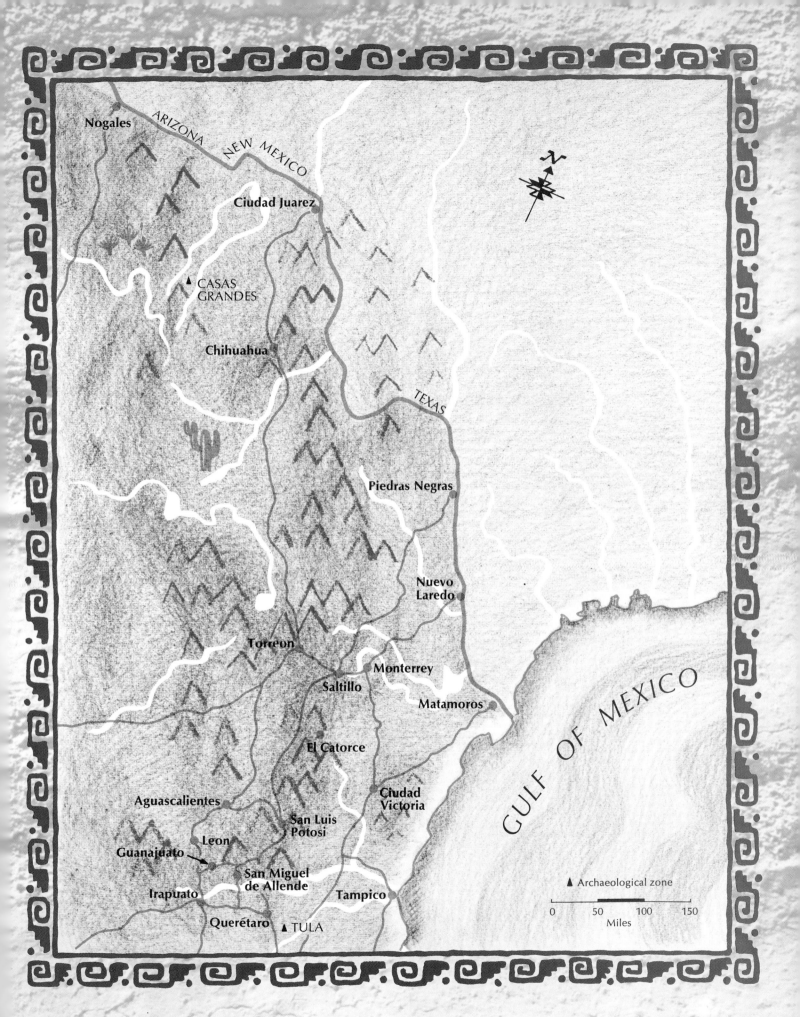

Nogales

ARIZONA

NEW MEXICO

Ciudad Juarez

▲ CASAS
GRANDES

Chihuahua

TEXAS

Piedras Negras

Nuevo
Laredo

Torreon

Monterrey

Saltillo

Matamoros

El Catorce

Ciudad
Victoria

Aguascalientes

San Luis
Potosi

Leon

Guanajuato

San Miguel
de Allende

Irapuato

Tampico

Querétaro   ▲ TULA

GULF OF MEXICO

▲ Archaeological zone

0   50   100   150
                Miles

CACTUS—MOST MEXICAN OF ALL NATIVE PLANTS

Only ten percent of Mexico's northern interior receives enough rain to grow crops year-round. Aside from its mineral wealth, this harsh land offered little to the Spaniards, so they used it chiefly as grazing country. Though greenery seems scarce in the vast desertlands of Sonora (above), Chihuahua, and Coahuila, hundreds of species of the ubiquitous cactus thrive in the searing sun. At right are shown some of the more common types seen in the north as well as deep in Mexico.

Barrel Cactus
Also known as *biznaga,* devil's pincushion, or compass plant (because it often slants south-west). Pulpy flesh stores considerable water. Height to 6 feet or more. Detail shows snaggable spines.

Prickly Pear
Also called *tuna.* This cactus is depicted (with eagle and snake) on Mexico's coat of arms. Fruit, shown in detail, is sweet, edible, sold in every market in Mexico. Height 10–12 feet.

HIGH AND DRY COUNTRY
Sparse Settlements...an Area to get through in a Hurry

"The great wasteland," northern Mexico has been called, ". . . a place to get through in a hurry." Settlements *are* few and far between; however, there is a rugged charm, a primitive pleasure to be derived from the desert country of the north. Visual rewards may be few, but the raw, natural beauty here is found in few other parts of the country.

LONG ASCENT to Mexico's Central Plateau is a hard haul in hot weather. At left, Highway 40 winds steadily uphill from Saltillo toward Torreon through rugged terrain, giving travelers from New Mexico or Texas a welcome relief from the flat landscape farther north.

Organpipe
Also called *organo, jarritos.* Slender, tall stems grow close together, reaching 10–20 feet. Rows of this cactus are grown as walls or fences. Detail shows harmonious star-shaped cross-section of trunk.

Cardón
Often called giant cactus. Ponderous branches rise from the trunk in a dense cluster to 50–60 feet. In spring, white flowers bloom. Detail shows wicked spear-shaped spine.

Saguaro
Another "giant" cactus, with weird humanoid form. Massive arms are favored woodpecker homes. Night blooming flowers are succeeded by fruit with supposedly aphrodisiac properties. Height to 50 feet.

CASAS GRANDES
Mysterious Big Houses just Below the Border

West of the main road connecting Ciudad Juarez and Chihuahua City lies an ancient ruined village that bears a striking resemblance to the Indian pueblos of the southwestern United States. Believed to have been built around 1200 A.D., the mysterious adobe town was possibly a trade crossroads, since shells found in the ruins are from the far-off Sea of Cortez.

A THRIVING CITY between about 800 and 1200 A.D., Casas Grandes had rooms, a water reservoir, structures that rose five stories high, opposite. Sweeping view above looks eastward across main interior court from a mound on which a temple stood. Plumed parrots were prized pets of the Indians. At night they were kept in covered adobe pens, left, which were closed with stone plugs. Their feathers were used for personal and ceremonial adornment.

Roadside crosses and piles of pebbles mark living memories

Some are scrolled ironwork, others are cast concrete, most are simply wood. They mark the scene of a highway tragedy. And each time friends or relatives pay a visit to the spot, to pray or simply to remember, they leave a small stone in loving memory.

Paper flowers and metal scrollwork

Living plants in rusty oil cans

Concrete cross on stump fencepost

Head of Christ within hare's head

Message of sorrow . . . and of love

A family of wooden crosses

Profile of Mexico
CANYON COUNTRY
Maybe not Deeper than Grand Canyon, but Every Bit as Magnificent

High in the northern Sierra Madre Occidental is an area of tumbled ridges, jutting buttes, and deep canyons. Some of the great earth trenches are nearly a mile deep and a mile across. A rail line runs through the big-canyon country from Ojinaga on the Texas-Mexico border to Los Mochis on the Pacific coast, but in most places the only way to explore this land is on foot or on horseback.

WILD MOUNTAINS and deep canyons of Mexico's north country support little agriculture, are thinly inhabited. At left, a small hay ranch huddles in the hills near Creel, Chihuahua. Above, an Indian plays flute in Copper Canyon.

The Tarahumaras: Fleet-Footed Hinterlanders of the Wild Sierra

Scattered throughout an immense area in the Sierra Madre Occidental are isolated communities of the Tarahumara Indian. Cautious, withdrawn, and wary of strangers, the Tarahumaras took refuge in the inhospitable back country when colonial settlers harrassed them, taking many into slavery. Early Jesuit missionaries brought a degree of Christianity, though, as with most primitive groups, the religion has undergone an adaptation to older pagan beliefs and practices.

One of the most sacred objects in the pantheon of the Tarahumaras is peyote, which they believe possesses the power to cure and bless. Even Christianized Indians place bits of the sacred cactus next to the image of a saint as double insurance. The name Tarahumara derives from the Spanish corruption of an Indian word meaning "foot runner." Noted for their stamina, the Tarahumaras think nothing of running non-stop for days at a time, and frequently pursue deer or rabbits to the point of the latter's exhaustion. Several men were entered as marathon runners in the 1928 Olympics but considered the 25-mile race a short jog, hardly worth trying for.

GRAPEFRUIT-SIZED BALL, whittled from gnarled branch, will be tossed out on rocky ground and kicked along by men running for as much as three days, until it is worn down to the size of a golf ball. Such foot races are usually highly organized, but sometimes just happen when several men feel like running. Women run too, opposite, but instead of kicking a ball, they fling a small hoop back and forth with sticks.

PRE-CHRISTIAN CUSTOMS make Tarahumara Easter ceremonies an extraordinary event. For a week the sound of drumming is heard around the clock. During the day, groups of painted men calling themselves "pharisees," above, dance, scream, and run around the church, trying to disrupt composure of officials within. On Holy Saturday, ceremony concludes with a straw Judas being brought to "trial," condemned, and burned.

MAIZE, OR CORN, is cultivated in small plots by the Tarahumaras, but its quality and quantity are low, since rain is scarce and in some years does not fall at all. Often erosion tears out entire plots, forcing groups of Indians to move to a different locale. In winter, the people head deep into the canyons of the Sierra to escape the bitter cold. Like the Huichols (page 56), the Tarahumaras hold peyote in high regard, believing that it possesses human attributes and the power to cure.

STONE HOUSES with dirt floors are the common Tarahumara dwelling in southern Chihuahua, whereas in the north the Indians live in caves. Clay cooking vessels are strictly utilitarian. The men carve primitive violins out of wood and make reed flutes but are not known for any native handicrafts.

CHIHUAHUA
A State, A Town, and the Memory of Pancho Villa

Capital of the state of the same name, Chihuahua is the first principal stopover on the road from Ciudad Juarez south, running along the backbone of Mexico. Largest city in northern Mexico, Chihuahua was the execution place of Miguel Hidalgo and other insurgents of the War of Independence. Historically, it has been the center of a vast ranching and mining district.

FRANCISCO
VILLA
1878 - 1923

CHIHUAHUA CATHEDRAL, opposite, is first major colonial structure seen by visitors driving south from El Paso on Highway 45. From its towers can be viewed the entire city, including the magnificent aqueduct. A monument of another sort is that of notorious revolutionary Pancho Villa, who sits astride his prancing horse on the northwest side of town. Villa's former Chihuahua home, one of the city's major tourist attractions, is maintained as a museum by one of his many wives. Cemetery monument, above, marks final resting place of Villa's body, minus head, in Hidalgo del Parral, south of Chihuahua City. After his initial burial in 1923, his grave was opened and the body decapitated. The present grave is enclosed in a firmly sealed vault.

Charreada is the aristocratic sport of Spanish-blooded gentlemen

DARING AND DANGEROUS event called coleada brings steer thundering out of corrals, above. Charro must grab bull's tail at full gallop, twist it around his leg, increase the speed of his mount, and thus flip the animal over on its back into a complete roll. The sooner a steer is thrown, the higher the rider's score. At right, a charro coolly sizes up animals in pens.

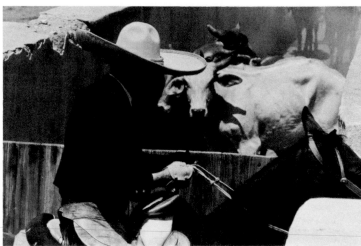

They may be only pretending to lasso a steer for the branding iron, or to rope a wild stallion, but they have to do it within strict rules and a tight time limit. Sire of the Wild West rodeo, the *charreada* or *jaripeo* places great demands on the skill and ability of Mexico's gentleman cowboy, who once worked as a ranch hand but who now rides and performs for the sheer joy of it.

FANCY ROPEWORK is a source of pride to charro, who has raised lasso handling from the usual cattle ranch activities to the level of a national sport. The huge sombrero must stay on through all of the strenuous activities; losing it loses points in a man's total score. Traditional show costume includes silver buttons, gold or silver embroidery, ornate spurs. Formal costume, confined to black with silver and white trim, is worn for balls and other formal events that take place on the ground or indoors.

EL CATORCE
Mining Town Frozen in Time

Given scarcely a word in popular guide books on Mexico, El Catorce, also known as Real de Catorce, is locally referred to as "that old place back in the hills." Like Zacatecas and Guanajuato, El Catorce began life as a mining town, but unlike the bigger cities, it passed into obscurity after the Revolution. Far off the regular tourist route, it is situated high in the mountains west of Matehuala, between Monterrey and San Luis Potosi.

TAILINGS from the old silver mines spill downhill behind town. When the city was in its heyday, riches flowing from the mines resulted in the building of opulent structures by affluent citizens. Catorce, meaning fourteen, supposedly received its name from a gang of local bandits numbering 14 who enjoyed rich pickings from the gentry. Though much of the city has been pilfered over the years by latter-day vandals, much of it remains as a living ghost town, a home for fewer than 200 people.

IRON FENCE backing up cast iron benches leans crazily into street, left, on which face once-elegant homes with yet-elegant balconies. Above, a wrought iron arch marking entry to a street is flanked by a winged dragon-like lighting fixture. Catorce is the site of Casa de Moneda (money house), where currency was minted up to the time of the 1910 Revolution.

MONTERREY
Industrial Center of the North Country

On one side of town is a gigantic steel mill that belches smoke and flame night and day as it turns out material for all of Mexico. On the other side of town is the country's largest brewery. In between are at least a thousand lesser factories, making this third largest city in Mexico its busy industrial hub.

CRAB-PINCHER PEAKS of Saddle Mountain, right, were created, according to a legend, by frantic digging of a local who lost a peso there, a story that reflects the supposed thrifty nature of the people of the north. Monterrey, famed as the home of the Cuauhtemoc Brewery, largest in Mexico, also produces glass, steel, cement, and automotive parts, which earns it the name of the Pittsburgh of Mexico. Monterrey has a bull ring, a charro ranch, a technical institute, modern hotels and motels. City growth and bustle are pointed out by monument of General Zaragoza, opposite, in sparkling Zaragoza plaza adjoining one of the city's newest hotels.

A Street Named the Fifth of May

Throughout Mexico there is an abundance of streets and avenues named after commemorative dates in history. Many are significant only locally; the following appear in almost every town in Mexico:

12 de Octubre. On October 12, 1492, Christopher Columbus first sighted land in the New World. The date celebrates the mingling of Spanish and Indian blood.

12 de Diciembre. On December 12, 1531, an Indian named Juan Diego had a vision of Mary, mother of Christ. The Virgin of Guadalupe became the patroness of all Mexicans.

21 de Marzo. This date marks the birth in 1806 of Benito Juarez, who became Mexico's first great liberal president.

16 de Septiembre. On September 16, 1810, Father Miguel Hidalgo y Costilla proclaimed Mexico's independence from Spain.

27 de Septiembre. On this date in 1821, Agustin Iturbide entered Mexico City, winning the war for independence from Spain.

5 de Mayo. On May 5, 1862, the invading French army was soundly defeated on the outskirts of Puebla.

20 de Noviembre. Francisco I. Madero declared the election of Porfirio Diaz null and void and called for a general insurrection to take place on November 20, 1910.

5 de Febrero. Constitution Day celebrates the promulgation of Mexico's present Magna Carta in 1917. On the same date in 1857, the country's first liberal constitution separating Church and state was proclaimed.

In Mexico, nothing is too big to carry

Before the wheel, man had hands, a head, and a strong back. In a land where changes come about gradually and gracefully, age-old habits persist, and hands and head sometimes remain the best way of transporting a block of ice or a basket of bakery goods.

BALANCING two heavy blocks of ice, a man hurries along before the early morning sun lightens his load; behind him a neighbor heads for the bakery, his hands full of basket. A pretty pastry vendor transports her entire store on her head, including brown-paper napkins.

FIVE BASKETS of bread are about maximum for one man and one bicycle, top, as they wobble along from bakery to store. Below, the bird man makes his way to market with a precarious load almost twice his height. Man at left has gathered a cargo of brush for door-to-door sale as firewood.

Discovery Town Well Off the Beaten Track

Northeast of San Miguel de Allende there was once a busy mining metropolis with a population of 40,000, a grand government palace, and a sturdy aqueduct. Today barely 200 people live there. The roof of the government building has long since fallen in. But the sturdy aqueduct still stands—a dry home for birds and mice.

WILDFLOWERS AND CACTUS grow in tumbled piles of stones, left, that once were part of wall next to church. Nearby, but out of picture, is an aqueduct that carried water to the town, and a grand house with a wide staircase, in the middle of which now flourishes a large pepper tree. Above, silent remains of a house stand on main street, the doorway choked with rubble. Delicate colors repeat blue of sky in lovely arches, opposite, which one present-day resident claims were part of "a school or the government building."

GUANAJUATO
Spanish Colonialism at its Very Best

Guanajuato was once a legendary mining center, supplying the world with silver and lead. Its narrow passageways echoed with the clatter of burros' hooves and boisterous laughter. The laughter is softer now, and the sound of hooves has been replaced by the wheeze of city buses as they gasp around the tortuous corners and grind up the precipitous hills.

JARDIN DE LA UNION is one of Mexico's finest plazas, with its Indian laurel trees, its fussy iron benches and lamps, its fairytale bandstand. Around it cluster fine, old hotels, the unbelievably romantic Teatro Juarez opera house, San Diego Church, shops, and a noisy, fun-filled soda fountain whose specialty is half a cantaloupe filled with rich ice cream.

"STREET WITH NO DOORS" is one of
the subterranean streets that were once
part of bed of Guanajuato River, which
is now diverted through the mountains.
Since streets are extremely narrow and
winding, walking is the best way to
explore and is rewarded by glimpses of
peeling doors, wood-barred windows,
ancient lights, all with the touch of
time on them.

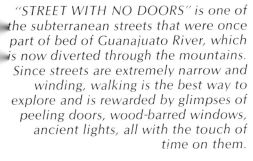

LIKE AN IVORY EGG, Guanajuato lies sheltered in a nest of velvet hills and mountains wherein run the once-rich veins of silver that made this the wealthiest city in silver-rich Mexico. A city steeped in history, Guanajuato was the scene of bloody fighting during the war of independence in 1810. After revolutionary leader Hidalgo was captured and executed in Chihuahua, his head was displayed in a cage hung from the walls of the local granary. Today the granary is a magnificent museum containing a moving shrine to the independence heroes, a display of folk arts and popular crafts, and an archaeological exhibit. The museum also houses one of the best appointed washrooms in Mexico.

ARTISTIC JEWEL, Valenciana Church sits on a hill about three miles out of town, facing the Valenciana Mine. Its facade displays beautiful stone filigree and horns of plenty as a testimony of bygone wealth. Its eye-dazzling altars have been described as "a flashing craziness of golds."

Corn is a basic need...a dietary obsession

SACRED SYMBOL of earth's bounty, a stalk of corn is carried reverently in a procession honoring a village patron saint, right. An ancient myth relates that after the failure of the gods to create man from elements of the earth, he was successfully given birth from corn. Portion of Diego Rivera mural in Mexico City's National Palace, above, shows Indians bartering corn.

Mexican life has been described as a culture surrounding a plant. It has also been said that Mexican life is based on corn, that the cause of the Revolution of 1910 was the long-stifled yearning of the people for land on which to grow corn. From ancient times corn has been so closely linked with human life in Mexico that the history of the two cannot be separated. From the date when Quetzalcoatl, god of life, transformed himself into a black ant so that he might enter the sacred hill of corn, this food has continued to be the staff of life to Mexico's millions.

SLAP, SLAP, SLAP rhythm of corn tortillas being patted out in the time-honored manner is sometimes drowned by the clanking screech of a mechanical assembly line. Even though tortillas are spoken of as "poor people's food," connoisseurs defend their virtues and claim that the thicker, uneven-textured ones, scorched on a piece of hot metal, are superior to those punched out paper thin and roasted evenly by a machine.

SAN MIGUEL DE ALLENDE
Colonial Ambience in a National Monument

"Perfect weather . . . peace and quiet . . . colonial ambience . . . a feeling of being at home . . ." These are some of the reasons Americans give for being attracted to San Miguel de Allende, a small town northwest of Queretaro. A place of textured walls and broken streets, grilled windows and wooden signs, clanging church bells and creaking doors, San Miguel exerts a mesmeric charm found in few small towns of the world.

THRUSTING UP from center of town, left, La Parroquia looks more a Gothic cathedral than the parochial Church of San Miguel. "Allende" was added to name in honor of Ignacio Allende, one of the patriots executed with Hidalgo in the struggle for independence against Spain. West of town lies a broad plain, the Laja River Valley.

PERSONALIZED DOORKNOCKERS and iron scrollwork adorn doors and windows, giving San Miguel the character that brought it fame and made it a national monument. Numerous hotels and restaurants offer modern conveniences, but in the interest of preserving the colonial atmosphere, all architecture and decor are in keeping with the town's picturesqueness. San Miguel is noted for its schools (see page 139), its market, and its fiestas, there seemingly being one or another celebration several times a month.

. . . San Miguel

SAN MIGUEL APPEALS TO AMERICANS because of its colonial charm, its pleasant climate, its aura of leisure, peace, and quiet. Nearby are such attractions as the historic Shrine of Atotonilco, a small, curious church whose inner walls and ceilings—every inch of them—are covered with paintings, decorations, inscribed prayers, and poetry. House and garden tours, left, offer chances to observe life behind the walls of some of the town's loveliest residences. View of La Parroquia, below, is from the sculpture garden of the Instituto Allende. Painting opposite shows unfinished sketches on a garden wall in the Institute.

San Miguel has a School for all Reasons

If you're looking for a place to spruce up your Spanish, hone your Latin American history, or liven your artistic leanings, San Miguel de Allende may be just the place. Along with its colonial charm and old-world architecture, this town has three schools that are highly regarded and popular with North Americans:

Academia Hispana Americana is one of Mexico's best schools for study of the Spanish language and literature. It also has a history and cultural department.

Instituto Allende is well known internationally, offers a stimulating array of courses ranging from arts and crafts to creative writing and Latin American literature. Former Palace of the Count of La Canal, the school offers students a hotel, apartments, theater, swimming pool, field trips, and numerous cultural activities.

The smallest and most informal school is Ignacio Ramirez Cultural Center. This giant, 18th century ex-convent is a captivating and genial center for instruction in arts and crafts as well as contemporary and pre-Hispanic art.

Most courses at the schools are in English. Most courses are also filled in advance and require reservations far ahead. For further information write directly to the respective school director at San Miguel de Allende, Guanajuato, Mexico.

Half a hint of hidden delights inside a home is often given by the personal touches seen on the front door. Some are utilitarian, others decorative—all are revealing to the curious and discerning eye. From the most humble, weather-worn panels to the precisely carved portals, from the hammered keyhole guard to the sawn letter drop, the doors of Mexico reflect the taste and the personality of those within.

Hammered metal keyhole

Wrought iron window grilles

Handcrafted letter drop

Tiled facing, carved panels

Front doors are a rich repository of local folk art

The fussy French touch

Delicately barred peep windows

Stylized serpent knocker

Simple slats and spools

ZOQUIZOQUIPAN is more easily found than pronounced, even though the village lies well off the beaten track. Not quite in the Mezquital Valley, Zoquizoquipan is near the town of Metztitlan, off Highway 105 connecting Tampico and Pachuca. Looking like a doll's castle, the late 16th century church-monastery balances on the precipitous edge of a deep canyon in the Sierra de Hidalgo, facing pine forests that rise in front of it. This is a little-explored part of Mexico, known for its tiny villages perched on mountain sides and its rugged terrain.

OTOMI COUNTRY
Two Hours and Three Centuries Away from the Capital

North of Mexico City is the mountainous state of Hidalgo, land of the shy Otomi Indian. Craggy country, little traversed by the ordinary traveler because of the lack of good roads, this picturesque region harbors hundreds of settlements that hardly warrant being called towns but which are home to numbers of gentle people who live close to the earth.

FORTRESS-MONASTERY of San Nicolas, built in 1546 as a mission in the land of the Otomi Indian, is in small town of Actopan, 70 miles north of Mexico City on the Pan-American Highway. Stone block walls are several feet thick; rooms are numerous and cavernous. Some stairways lead down into darkness, ending at a solid wall. Steps are worn to a diagonal at their edges by the passage of millions of feet.

Maguey provides many people with all the necessities of life

OTOMI INDIAN spins dried fibers that have been stripped from maguey leaves, then weaves the threads into a coarse fabric, using a loom that she wears like a belt. Opposite, a tlachiquero and his young helper plod home after siphoning aguamiel (literally, sweet water), a liquid that collects in the heart of the maguey, which will be fermented to make pulque, a mild intoxicant.

The Aztecs wrote on paper made from its leaves and became euphoric by drinking fermented juices gathered from its heart. Indians used it for fencing and roofing, for needle and thread, for twine and fabric, and they wore its thorns for religious penitence. In the back country its historic uses endure, while in modern research centers it is being studied as a source of industrial, nutritive, and medical products. Maguey, family *Agavaceae,* is one of the most versatile plants in all of the Americas.

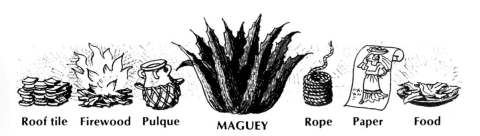

Roof tile Firewood Pulque **MAGUEY** Rope Paper Food

MAGUEY HAS MANY USES
Practical as well as hardy, the maguey historically has been an essential part of the culture of the people of the Mezquital Valley. The "century plant" is related to that which produces tequila and henequen.

TULA
Lost Capital
of the Ancient Toltec

The stone warriors stand in silent splendor atop a low pyramid overlooking the town of Tula, some fifty miles northwest of Mexico City. Although every bit as impressive as other ruins, the legendary city of Tollan has comparatively few visitors. It is a place where one can quietly commune with the spirits of ancient peoples and their gods.

COLOSSAL WARRIORS are believed to have been columns that supported temple roof atop a five-tiered pyramid during peak of Toltec culture. From about 900 to 1000 A.D. Tula was the main ceremonial center of the Toltecs (see page 13). Legend spoke of the ancient capital, but for centuries no one knew where it was until late in the 19th century when a French treasure hunter and soldier of fortune stumbled on traces of it. Not until 1940, and again in 1950, were excavations made proving it to be a major archaeological site. Warrior figures guarded the principal entrance to main temple of the Pyramid of Tlahuizcalpantecuhtli. He was of the House of Dawn, which is a fine time to experience the ruin and ponder the pronunciation of his name.

CHACMOL, left, was a heavenly messenger, his destination defined by the type of offering placed in his belly receptacle. Although usually associated with the far off Yucatan, chacmols found in Tula helped to establish a relationship between the late Maya and Toltec civilizations. After 1000 A.D., traders and immigrant groups affected an exchange of cultural elements between central highlands and the Yucatan, resulting in notable similarities. Magnificent head below shows facial detail of warrior.

BOLD BAS RELIEFS decorating base of pyramid of Temple of Lord of the Dawn were once painted in brilliant colors but now have weathered to the natural gray of the stone. From left to right: a feasting vulture; a human face intertwined with eagles; a jaguar wearing a collar.

HEIGHT OF WARRIORS—Tula's most outstanding feature—is sixteen feet. They are made of interlocking, mortised, drumlike sections. Figures wear feathered headdress, apron, sandals, and belt with a clasp symbolizing the sun. In one hand they have a dart thrower, in the other a bundle of darts, indicating that the Toltec culture was chiefly a militaristic society. Toltec civilization gradually gave way to the more powerful Aztecs, who controlled all of the central highlands.

Comemos: We eat, we are eating

It's not that Mexicans eat a *lot;* it's just that they are always eating. Maybe it has to do with the fact that they are not self-conscious about partaking in public. Maybe it's because they consume small amounts often, rather than indulge in a lot at once. Maybe it's simply because they are constantly surrounded with mounds of good food.

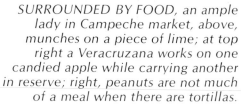

SURROUNDED BY FOOD, an ample lady in Campeche market, above, munches on a piece of lime; at top right a Veracruzana works on one candied apple while carrying another in reserve; right, peanuts are not much of a meal when there are tortillas.

FOLD-YOUR-OWN TACOS require deft handling, left, and a plate held close under but well away from the body, especially when standing up in fancy dress. The senorita below happily crunches a slab of chicharon, crisp pork fat, while keeping an inquisitive eye on her audience.

Mexico

"We Saw Such

THE AIR OF MEXICO CITY is thin, but it is highly charged with change and contradiction. Almost 650 years after its founding, the capital is still growing in all directions, still in a state of ceaseless agitation, still a mixture of ideas and ideals. Streets are not regimented by a regular grid pattern but run wildly in all directions, impatiently switching their names every few blocks. Settlements that are suburbs one day are ingested by the city and become *colonias* the next. Aunt Jemima's Pancake House competes with Colonel Sanders' Kentucky Fried Chicken and Denny's Coffee Shop. "We are losing our identity," proclaims an insurance salesman, chewing on a pastrami sandwich.

Pedestrians charge in and out of traffic, dodging cold metal as skillfully as a matador eludes a hot-blooded bull. Vendors fretfully thrust brilliant flowers and colorful lottery tickets into car windows. Automobile horns bleat out "Mary Had a Little Lamb," in ear-bending tones. "We are in too much of a hurry," shouts a taxi driver, changing lanes abruptly.

In front of the Cathedral, old women sell religious postcards and young men hawk wristwatches, toy helicopters, and instant portraits. "We are not respectful," says a priest, as he licks a chocolate-covered ice cream bar.

At the Saturday Market in San Angel, the music is pure Mexican, the buffet Continental, the drinks North American, the languages French, Dutch, and German. "We forget how to speak our native tongue," says a native artisan, in English.

Along Paseo de la Reforma, skyscrapers grow upward to the tune of jack hammers and rivet guns, as once again the old is thrown to the ground and the new rises in its place. Half-completed buildings stand as empty monuments to architecture, as tributes to overbuilding. "We are too hasty," a bank executive declares, jabbing the elevator button for the third time.

City

Wondrous Sights..."

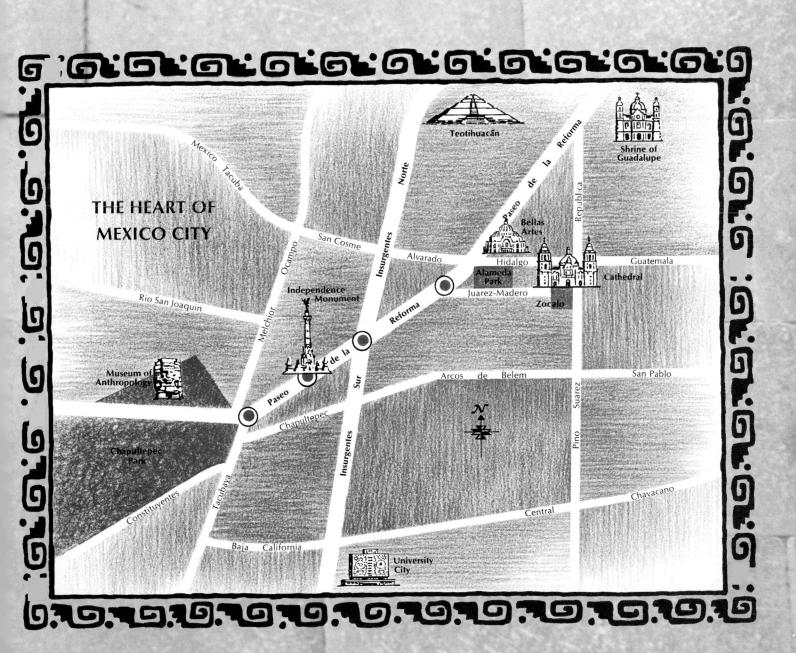

THE HEART OF MEXICO CITY

Teotihuacán

Shrine of Guadalupe

Mexico Tacuba

Norte

Paseo de la Reforma

San Cosme

Republica

Ocampo

Insurgentes

Alvarado

Bellas Artes

Independence Monument

Rio San Joaquin

Hidalgo

Guatemala

Melchior

Reforma

Juarez-Madero

Cathedral

Alameda Park

Zocalo

Museum of Anthropology

Paseo de la

Sur

Arcos de Belem

San Pablo

Chapultepec

Suarez

N

Chapultepec Park

Insurgentes

Pino

Tacubaya

Chavacano

Constituyentes

Central

Baja California

University City

THE ZOCALO
Kilometer Zero of Mexico

The word signifies a public square, and there is one in every Mexican town. But Mexico City's Zocalo is the political and religious center of the republic, the geographical point from which all highway distances to the capital are measured. Heart of the nation since 1325, when the Aztecs founded their empire near the present site of the Cathedral, the Zocalo has been witness to the flowing tides of humanity and history for more than six centuries.

BARE EXPANSE and blank immensity of Mexico's main plaza are usually a surprise to first-time visitors. Area was once a lovely park filled with trees, but they were removed during revolutionary days because they blocked aim of guns bombarding palace. Cathedral, opposite, is built on remains of the great Aztec temple. Portions of it lean crazily—a testimony to its sheer bulk and the former lake bed on which it sits. Office of President and other government bureaus are housed in National Palace, below. Over the central entrance (marked by bare flagpole) hangs the liberty bell, rung by President each September 15, Mexico's Day of Independence. Mural, left, by Diego Rivera, is one of many decorating walls of National Palace.

LOVE FOR COLOR and fun is evidenced in glow of Cathedral (above), government buildings, and main streets decorated for special holidays. During such times, throngs jam the Zocalo, dressed in fantastic costumes, singing, shouting, and letting loose their emotions. Large hat on man, right, is not merely part of his costume; it's to protect his hair from handfuls of flour hurled about in gleeful abandon.

COMPARATIVE QUIET in the Zocalo means that the noise of surging traffic has settled down to a dull roar, a modulation that happens only briefly in the wee hours of the morning, below. Metro station of nearby Pino Suarez, left, contains grand relic of quieter days. During tunneling for the subway, workers unearthed an Aztec pyramid. Rather than destroy such a national treasure, engineers restored the pyramid and built the subway station around it.

MADERO-JUAREZ
Culture, Relaxation, and Magnificent Murals

Madero-Juarez Avenue is a surging stream of pedestrians and automobiles, a river whose banks are crammed with buildings, federal offices, restaurants, and hotels. The avenue boasts one of the city's finest parks, one of the country's best performing arts centers, a tiled restaurant built as a home by a profligate son, a church where Cortes attended Mass, a palace that once housed an emperor, and the tallest building in Latin America.

JUAREZ AVENUE, a handsome boulevard, fronts Palace of Fine Arts (lower right corner of photo) and length of Alameda Park. Along Juarez are several of the capital's finest older hotels, as well as small stores and shops jammed tightly together. Serpentine building at end of Alameda Park is the Crystal Palace Bookstore, which has outlets in several major cities. The luxuriant growth of trees in Alameda Park is attributed to the fact that it was the burial place for thousands who were executed by order of the tribunal during the Spanish Inquisition of 1575.

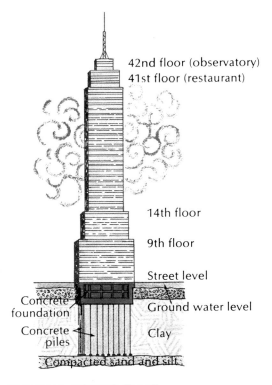

SINKING CITY is an apt appellation for Mexico City, where some buildings along Madero-Juarez are settling at an alarming rate, left, because of the pudding-like nature of the soil. The Latin American Tower, seen below from Alameda Park, has a "floating" foundation which keeps it stable even during severe earthquakes.

42nd floor (observatory)
41st floor (restaurant)

14th floor

9th floor

Street level

Concrete foundation

Ground water level

Concrete piles

Clay

Compacted sand and silt

THE TALL TOWER THAT FLOATS ON MUD
A prototype of buildings constructed in seismic areas, the Latin American Tower design is based on three principles: compensation by excavation—same amount of soil was removed as building weighs; pilot columns that balance rather than anchor; flotation of concrete foundation.

. . . Madero-Juarez

WORLD CATASTROPHE is theme of huge Orozco mural, a graphic indictment of the evils of over-mechanization. Rifles symbolize terrible effects of war on progress of mankind, but in the presence of such holocaust nothing daunts the eternal female. Since pre-Columbian times, murals have been a means of education and propagandizing. This is one of several works in the upper galleries of Bellas Artes by Orozco, Tamayo, Siquieros, Rivera, and others. The large, squat building, constructed east of Alameda Park under dictator-president Porfirio Diaz, also houses the world-renowned Ballet Folklorico, the symphony, and the opera.

MONUMENT TO INDEPENDENCE, the Juarez Hemicycle, left, grandly faces Juarez Avenue at edge of Alameda Park. In a country of monuments, this marble edifice is one of the finest. Diego Rivera mural, above, in lobby of Del Prado Hotel has smiling death fashionably attired for a Sunday stroll. With frog and snake in his pockets, the artist as a youth holds death's bony hand; behind him stands an unsmiling Frida Kahlo, his wife. The mural depicting pre-Revolution days was once curtained off from public view because of an antireligious motto that was subsequently removed.

Loteria Nacional: Cash prizes
from the Goose that Lays the Golden Egg

YOUTHFUL PRIDE is evident in manner of uniformed lads who perform drawings. Marked balls drop from two large revolving cages—one for the winning ticket, the other for the amount of prize. Numbers are sung out at full lung power. Audiences for drawings are welcome; lottery building is at Juarez Avenue and Paseo de la Reforma.

You may disapprove of it but you can't ignore it, for like mariachi music, the National Lottery of Mexico is everywhere all the time. It is a pastime that can become a passion, an avocation that can become an obsession. It is a kind of Mexican madness that possesses chance-minded individuals from Tijuana to Tapachula, from Matamoros to Isla Mujeres. You can buy a *billete entero,* a whole ticket, if you feel expansive, or any of its 25 parts if you're the cautious type. You could win a couple of pesos or thousands of dollars.

DID I WIN? Hopeful eyes scrutinize winning numbers posted outside a tobacco shop, left. Tickets can be purchased from such shops—some are titled "The Goose that Lays the Golden Egg"—or from sidewalk vendors who pop up waving tickets in the most remote parts of the republic, above. Tickets come in varying amounts, the cost being determined by the size of the prize, which can amount to several million pesos. Profits are used for charitable institutions.

PASEO DE LA REFORMA
Monuments and Monumental Traffic Jams

Mexico City's stately boulevard, one of the loveliest streets in the world, is a remembrance of France left by Emperor Maximilian. Desiring a direct route between Chapultepec Castle and the mid-town part of the capital, he modeled the thoroughfare after Paris' Champs-Elysees. Bold architecture is replacing much of Reforma's aged buildings, but the transition is gradual, and fine old homes rub elbows with glass-fronted towers, blending Mexico's yesterday with its tomorrow.

A BROAD BOULEVARD with expansive sidewalks, tall trees, and landscaped plots, left, the Reforma invites strollers and sitters. Along its length in the downtown area are highrise hotels, theaters, embassies, restaurants, and countless statues of illustrious men. Set in circular plazas (glorietas) in the middle of the parkway, major monuments soar skyward. Best known is the Angel of Independence, opposite, who was toppled from her 150-foot column by an earthquake in 1957 but who once again spreads her golden wings as a symbol of Mexico. Simply by being in the way, the glorietas help regulate Reforma's turbulent river of traffic, but there are times when it comes to a dead halt, above, and the sound of screeching tires is replaced by the deafening din of horns.

EL CABALLITO, "Little Horse," is euphemistic name given to massive equestrian statue of Charles IV, King of Spain, standing at intersection of Paseo de la Reforma and Juarez Avenue. It is said that the statue is tolerated because of the horse, not because of the rider. In background is the new lottery building.

Mexico City Means Monuments

Mexico City's landscape is punctuated with monuments. Works of art in their own right, they are also useful as orienting landmarks to the visitor, especially the six along central Paseo de la Reforma:

The Little Horse. The monument to Charles IV (see photo above), located at Juarez and Guerrero Avenues, is reputed to be the second largest bronze sculpture in the world.

Columbus Monument. This large group, at Versalles and Ignacio Ramirez, includes statues of four priests who aided Columbus.

Monument to Cuauhtemoc. At Re-

forma and Insurgentes is the massive monument memorializing the last Aztec emperor.

Diana Fountain. At Lieja Avenue, Diana draws her bronze bow above the entrance to Chapultepec Park.

Independence Monument. At Rio Tiber and Florencia, the Little Angel column rises from grassy terraces, a favorite place for parade watchers.

Simon Bolivar Monument. Last of the major monuments on the Reforma, the hero of Latin America sits astride his horse a block west of the entrance to Chapultepec Park.

THREE ERAS are manifestly evident at Tlatelolco, the Plaza of Three Cultures, a block west of Paseo de la Reforma at Cuitlahuac monument. Here rise an architecturally modern group of apartment buildings; the Church of Santiago, built in 1524 for sons of Aztec nobles; and the remains of the great ceremonial center and pyramid, where Cuauhtemoc, last great Aztec emperor, made his final stand against Cortes. A plaque speaks of the date August 13, 1521, as ". . . neither a triumph nor a defeat but the painful birth of the hybrid that is the Mexico of today."

LEFT BANK of Paris, Rome's Via Veneto, London's Carnaby Street don't outglitter Mexico City's Zona Rosa (Pink Zone), also called Niza District (after one of its principal streets), and Credit Card Row. This high-fashion area is in the heart of the main hotel area, close to Paseo de la Reforma.

ZONA ROSA
Swinging Shops in the Leggiest Part of Town

What started out a few years ago as a collection of intimate shops with an "in" flavor has now blossomed like a rose into a full-blown area where just about everything worthwhile in today's mod world can be seen, heard, or bought. Bounded by Paseo de la Reforma, Insurgentes Avenue, Chapultepec, and Florencia, the district has the highest concentration of bistros, boutiques, and short skirts in the capital.

PINK ZONE is name supposedly given area by famous painter who claimed the light was a glowing color. Anything is likely to be seen here, whether it be a city employee dutifully painting the trees shocking pink or a vintage automobile garlanded with flowers, peering from the upper floor of an exclusive shop.

Machismo means that it's a man's world

The strongest and most intimate wish of the Mexican male is to be *muy macho,* utterly virile. The *macho* is masculinity personified; his goal is to be forceful, brave, aggressive, invulnerable, scornful of danger and death. Mexican sociologists agree that *machismo* conceals a delicate sense of inferiority that harks back to the subjugation of the Conquest.

INDIFFERENCE TO DEATH is implicit in taunting of the bulls, above, as it is in the highly respected profession of matador; a wound is proof positive of daring to be a man. The cantina, or saloon, right, is strictly male territory. It is the macho's sacrosanct retreat where he is free to drink strong liquor, weep over the world's injustices, and discuss the women — both real and imaginary — in his life.

BRAVERY AND VALOR in the face of danger are all wrapped up in the figure of the charro, above, who must be a superb horseman and have little regard for his own limbs. The gun, with its power of life or death, and the mustache are both physical symbols of force, power, and maleness.

THE MARKETPLACE
Ever Since the Aztecs, an Unbelievable Variety

Onions and oranges rise in tidy pyramids as tall as one's shoulders; fabrics and leather goods are stacked in neat piles; pottery and baskets lie next to ribbons and flowers, love potions next to turkeys and chickens. The sounds are exciting, the smells intriguing, the diversity endless. With something for everyone, the market is a life force, a meeting place for all strata of Mexico.

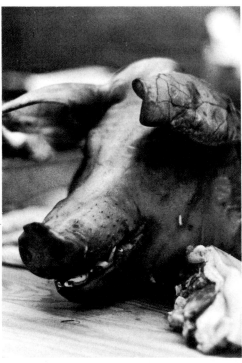

PYRAMIDS OF PRODUCE and a grinning pig's head tempt shoppers in the city's frenetic food markets. Among the largest and busiest markets in the capital are Merced (produce, meats), San Juan (flowers, foods, handicrafts), Jamaica (pottery, toys, baskets, herbs).

"HOW CAN I GET IT HOME?" seems to be the question pondered by lady at far left. Bizarre objects and displays are characteristic of Lagunilla (also referred to as Thieves' Market) and the Market of Curiosities, both rich repositories of what some call junk, others call treasures. Spirited bargaining is in order, and tasteful haggling is respected.

CHAPULTEPEC PARK
The Old and the New on Grasshopper Hill

The ahuehuete trees nurtured by the Aztecs are majestic; the castle built by a Spanish viceroy is romantic; the red mill that was the scene of a bloody skirmish of the Mexican-American War is picturesque. The "old" park is 700 years old, the "new" is less than a decade. Like all of Mexico, Chapultepec Park is a marvelous blend of antiquity and modernity.

RANGE OF ATTRACTIONS offered by fabulous park includes theaters, museums, zoo, boating, botanical gardens, concerts, restaurants, the Presidential home, and a real castle. Stylized Indian fountain at right is one of several magnificent water displays in this playground of the people, where balloon vendors, opposite, enjoy their greatest glory on weekends.

"GRASSHOPPER HILL" is meaning of Chapultepec, a name given by the Aztecs, who used area for a zoo and summer residence for royalty. Above, Chapultepec Castle stands on a high hill, has been a military school, a palace (Maximilian and Carlota), a presidential residence. It now houses the National Museum of History.

MUSEUM OF ANTHROPOLOGY
A Pleasure…an Experience…
a Marvelous Record of Mexico

Its official name is The National Museum of
Anthropology; its purpose—to house artifacts
and exhibits of Mexico's art, archaeology,
and ethnography. But such formal titles and aims
inadequately describe this museum among museums,
this living record of the life and times of a race of people
whose glory reaches back eight thousand years to the
first creative testimony of Mesoamerican culture.

*"THEY BEGAN TO TEACH THEM: How
to live, how to respect people, how to
submit to what is right and just . . .
they are to avoid wrong, fleeing with
strength from evil, perversion, and
greed." The words of an ancient king
set the tone of visual drama and
emotional impact of this finest of
anthropological and cultural museums.*

"COMENZABAN A ENSEÑARLES:
COMO HAN DE VIVIR.
COMO HAN DE RESPETAR A LAS PERSONAS.
COMO SE HAN DE ENTREGAR A LO CONVENIENTE Y RECTO,
HAN DE EVITAR LO MALO.
HUYENDO CON FUERZA DE LA MALDAD.
LA PERVERSION Y LA AVIDEZ"
HUEHUETLATOLLI

CURTAIN OF WATER cascades from umbrella roof in central patio. Bronze relief sculpture by Chavez Morado decorates central column, depicts major events in Mexican history. At opposite end of courtyard is a reflecting pool, a sculptured conch shell that mournfully sounds the hour, and a ceremonial brazier in which is ignited a symbolic fire. First floor of museum contains archaeological exhibits of the Mesoamerican cultures, including the Veracruz, Oaxaca, and Maya areas, as well as northern and western Mexico. Second floor has ethnological exhibits, with complete dwellings.

MAIN TEMPLE OF HOCHUB, in state of Campeche, is reproduced full-scale in a jungle setting adjacent to the museum building. Such outdoor exhibits provide variety and a pleasant change from the inside displays. Also outside are giant stone heads from La Venta (Tabasco), and a Tarascan Indian house.

AZTEC SUN STONE dramatically dominates Mexica Room, above, which is dedicated to displaying the civilization of the Aztecs. Figure in foreground is Coatlicue, goddess of birth and death; her serpent skirt symbolizes the earthbound character of human life. A casual eye could almost be fooled by the near-reality of ethnographic exhibits, left. The mushroom-shaped structure is an authentic Nahua granary.

CENTRAL LIBRARY is covered on all four sides with an incredibly complex and beautiful mosaic mural by Juan O' Gorman that depicts the history of Mexico from pre-Columbian times. Main reading rooms of the library are windowless, but light is admitted as a soft glow through a native marble, called tecali, that is sliced extremely thin. University City contains on one campus the many schools of the oldest university in North America. Before 1950 buildings of the university had been located all over Mexico City.

Profile of Mexico
UNIVERSITY CITY
Five Hundred Acres Devoted to Learning

A grand complex of starkly modern buildings, a collage of soaring steel and glass structures resting on ancient lava beds, Mexico's National University draws students from the world over. The library building has been photographed so much that its image has come to stand for Mexico. The theme of this institute of higher education is appropriately depicted in one of its murals: "The people go to the university, and the university goes to the people."

FOOTBALL in large courtyard at end of School of Medicine, left, provides welcome respite from studies. Eppens' mosaic mural "Life and Death" symbolizes birth of the mestizo, the Mexican derived from Spanish and Indian forbearers. Above, youngsters delight in climbing the bold Rivera mosaic executed on University Stadium at west end of campus across Insurgentes Avenue.

Iron work insures that a man's home is his castle

"No Parking," San Angel District

Barred balcony doors, Tacuba

Modest window, Mixcoac District

High fence in driveway, San Rafael

Iron bars may not make a cage, but in Mexico grillework and high walls are more than physical safeguards or decorative fineries. They are a mark of success, a sign of cultural monopoly. In the republic's central plateau, where external appearances are all-important, a man can hide securely behind his manners—and the bars on his windows.

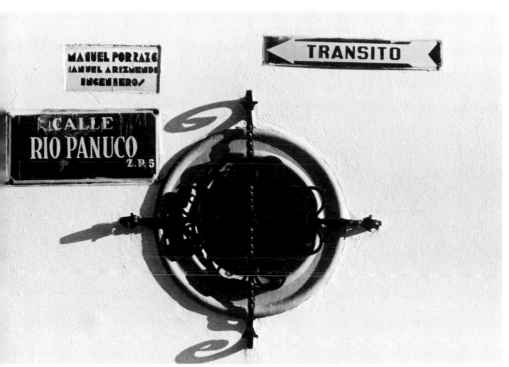

Porthole, engineer's residence, San Rafael

Simplicity in frosted glass, Tlalpan

Modern steel garage door, Guerrero

White clover design, San Angel

REFRESHMENT BARGE bumps up to Rosita, family filled and festive. Xochimilco's flat-bottomed launches are available in sizes holding from one to 20 people, the cost per hour depending on the size. The flowered arches were once made with real blossoms but now are plastic—a concession to modern times. Even with all the gay sounds of lusty mariachi bands, singing picnickers, and colliding boats, the rides along the canals are pleasantly peaceful. It is customary to offer the hard-working pole boy a soft drink, but as one sagacious observer admonishes, don't offer him liquor or you may have to pole yourself back.

Profile of Mexico
XOCHIMILCO
On Sunday, it's Flowers, Fun, and Floating Bands

Although most Americans claim it is dirty and depressing, most Mexicans consider it to be one of the very best places near the capital for a Sunday outing. Made up of equal parts of excitement, confusion, and hilarity, the floating gardens (which aren't really gardens, and don't really float) are not as much a place to look at as they are a spectacle to be experienced.

"PHOTO, SENOR?" A photographer's boat slips between a launch and the cypress-lined shore, above. Centuries ago the islands were immense wicker baskets, filled with earth, that actually floated and on which crops were planted. When roots grew into the lake bed the islands became permanently anchored. At left, a lady in a flower-laden canoe offers her colorful wares.

Sitting is an art that requires plenty of practice

Living may sometimes become tedious, but in few other places of the world are its inevitabilities accepted with the grace they are accorded in Mexico. As the stream of life eddies about him, the Mexican can momentarily disregard both the strength and the direction of the current.

WHY STAND when you can sit? Two cronies take their ease curbside, above, and reminisce about better days while waiting for the local bus. At right, a street sweeper rests his twig broom and himself long enough to unwrap and enjoy a leisurely breakfast.

WHY SIT when you can lie down? Drying nets, above left, droop in a manner suggestive of repose, so between mendings a fisherman reposes. Oblivious to activity around her, a vendor of religious articles, above, catches a nap between Masses. It's going to be a long day, left, so what better way to begin it than with a snooze on a park bench.

SHRINE OF GUADALUPE
Solemnity and Gaiety at the Spiritual Center of the Nation

Nowhere else in the Western world is religious dedication so manifest. The winds of faith waft so strongly through the Basilica, the chapels, and the shrines that they can be felt. The earnestness of the believers is mute testimony to their devotion. Yet beneath the solemnity is a holiday air that makes the irrepressible Mexican's religion a thing of earthy reality.

REVERENT PILGRIMS drop to knees at entrance gate facing Basilica, then laboriously crawl across the great plaza. The ordeal is made as a penance or to fulfill a promise made for favors received. Guadalupe is site of vision of the Virgin by an Indian convert in 1531, a phenomenon that was instrumental in the conversion of millions of Indians to Christianity.

RATTLES AND BELLS accompany ceremonious Indian dancers, left, performing in front of Basilica in honor of both Christian and Aztec deities. More holiday in nature is the mood of happy visitors being photographed on steps up Tepeyac Hill behind Basilica, below. At top of hill are a chapel, souvenir stands, and snack shops. Halfway up is a somewhat incongruous object—a large Spanish galleon under full sail, executed in gilded concrete. It was constructed in memory of a miracle, attributed to the Virgin, in the Gulf of Mexico.

TEOTIHUACAN
Where Men Become Gods

Teotihuacan had been a deserted ruin for more than 500 years when the Aztecs came upon it. The site's colossal structures and spacious thoroughfares led them to believe that the ancient city had been the home of giants, who must have been god-like to have constructed such an awe-inspiring center. In the words of an ancient text, "Before there was light . . . the gods met, there in Teotihuacan." The grandeur that was Teotihuacan still exists, and indeed it is a place where one feels akin to the gods.

AVENUE OF THE DEAD, left, stretches for 1 mile from Plaza of the Moon, foreground, is faced along both sides with temples and courtyards that were used for various religious ceremonies. Large, dark mass to left of avenue is Pyramid of the Sun (opposite page), once the base of a temple. The pyramid is 213 feet high, its long-slanting sides and staircase that narrows as it ascends toward the top enhance the feeling of height.

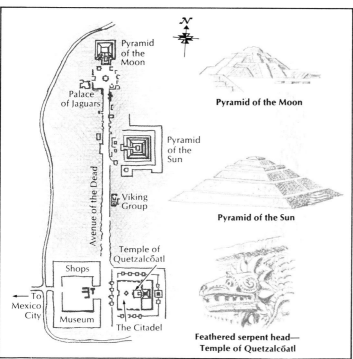

Pyramid of the Moon

Pyramid of the Sun

Feathered serpent head—
Temple of Quetzalcóatl

TEOTIHUACAN—THE PLANNED CITY
Teotihuacan's most important structures are situated on a north-south axis. As seen today, the ruins are only the ceremonial center of the original city, which covered an area of more than 40 square miles. The archaeological zone is but a short drive on good highway north from Mexico City.

ENERGETIC CLIMBERS ATOP Pyramid of the Sun, above, appear as mere dots against the sky. The long climb up takes strong legs, good breath, and stamina. Stone steps are narrow, steep, and high, and the altitude leaves even the best climbers puffing. View above is across Avenue of the Dead.

DINERS TAKE THEIR EASE in the fine
restaurant at the visitor center, left.
Pyramid of the Moon is in the distance,
at end of the Avenue of the Dead.
Below, a curious sight-seer explores
mouth of Quetzalcoatl, the feathered
serpent that figured prominently in
several early Mexican cultures.

Religion has many faces, all of them serious

SAINT SANTIAGO is venerated, above, in a ceremony involving the lighting of tiny candles and the burning of sweet-smelling incense in a pagan/Christian ceremony in the highlands of Chiapas. At right, despite gay decoration, confetti, and deafening music, participants in a Guadalajara procession maintain a solemn composure.

Christianity arrived with the Spaniards. Replacing pagan beliefs and practices, it became a sober religion based more on duty than on conviction, more on guilt than on joy. A wariness of unknown natural forces was supplanted by the specter of eternal retribution. Sacrifice was replaced with self-immolation. Though the majority of Mexico's people are Christianized, this Christianity is an odd mixture of old and new whose roots reach far back into the dim past.

VENERABLE WOMEN pray as a group, left, at culmination of a wearying pilgrimage to the Basilica of Guadalupe in Mexico City. Woman above adds a votive candle to the hundreds already flickering—a common sight at most of Mexico's churches.

East to

A Living

CORTES AND HIS CONQUISTADORS took twelve weeks to work their way from the coast to the capital. As the jet flies, Veracruz is scarcely an hour from Mexico City, and motorists can travel the distance in less than a day. Still, the Spaniards started it all when they established a travel corridor that has been in constant use for some 450 years.

Between Mexico City and Puebla the road is a fast, multi-lane *cuota* (tollway) that rises swiftly out of the Valley of Mexico. Once it begins its long, smooth descent toward Puebla through pine foothills, it is an introduction to the spectacular scenery that characterizes the route the rest of the way to the coast.

Everywhere in Puebla life is frantic, but the greatest activity is centered around the Zocalo, with its arcades filled with restaurants, sidewalk cafes, candy shops, and people. Although Puebla is known for its ornate architecture and colorful tiles, the most impressive ceramic work is on the churches of Cholula, just west of the city.

Between Puebla and Orizaba the road drops from 7000 feet to 4000 feet and stays near that elevation, giving the motorist the feeling that he is driving along just under the sky. Views of Popocatepetl and Ixtaccihuatl are replaced by one of mighty Orizaba, also called Citlaltepetl — Mountain of the Star — Mexico's highest peak, snow-capped and soaring to an elevation of almost 19,000 feet.

From Orizaba east, the way is all downhill, through plantations of coffee and tobacco, through acres of orchids and azaleas, bananas and oranges, papayas and pineapples.

The road ends at the Gulf of Mexico, at Veracruz, the place where Cortes began his long march of conquest. Then it was a quiet beach and empty swampland. Now it is bright, noisy, and lively, one of the most exciting cities in the Western Hemisphere.

the Gulf
Link with Spain

Archaeological zone

0   50   100   150
Miles

N

GULF OF MEXICO

Pachuca

Ixtaccíhuatl

Malinche   Jalapa

Mexico City

Puebla   Pico de
Orizaba

Veracruz

Popocatépetl

Orizaba

Laguna de Términos

Isla del Carmen

Villahermosa

PALENQUE

THE MONASTIC TRAIL
Historical Side Trip South of the Capital

Southeast of Mexico City off the busy tollway to Puebla is Highway 115, a prosaic appellation for a sizeable segment of Mexico's colonial past. Though only some fifty miles in length, the winding road passes through picturesque small towns and gives onto dusty byways little noted on road maps. Best of all, it yields access to a chain of early churches and monasteries.

PLEASANT PATIO is where people wait patiently to see parish priest at Tlalmanalco's 16th century Church of San Luis Obispo, above. Cloisters have ornate frescoes, elaborately incised arches. Church at Chalco, right, is not on the main plaza but next to it. Exterior is carved stone and red block; inside are lovely blue, yellow, and green tiles, waist-high on the walls.

HIGH ON A HILL, to the west of Highway 115, up an ankle-deep-in-dust road that gives way near the top to ankle-breaking cobblestones, is the church of Tepetlixpa, left. Inside, under its dome, are four saints, each in a curious mode of locomotion. Church of Yecapixtla, below, rests massively two miles east of road, frowning like a medieval fortress. Above its front portal is a fine, pierced rose window; around the entry are empty niches—where have all the saints gone?

Monastery-Convent
Characteristics: squarish narrow building connected to priests' quarters; walled courtyard; cloisters; roof merlons (see detail).

Cathedral
Characteristics: massive construction; numerous side chapels; towers; domes; rose window (see detail).

Parish Church
Characteristics: usually modest-sized; varies from spartan buildings to scrollwork structures with ornate crosses (see detail).

HOW TO TELL A CATHEDRAL FROM A MONASTERY
The 16th, 17th, and 18th centuries marked an era of frenzied church construction all over Mexico; during this colonial period, some 12,000 churches were built. Many of them still remain as a valuable part of Mexico's heritage.

NATURAL WONDERS
Mountain Magnificence of Mexico's Oldest Travel Corridor

Geographers refer to Mexico's volcanic axis, a vast east-to-west highland of ragged volcanic peaks with rugged names such as Popocatepetl, Ixtaccihuatl, Malinche, and Orizaba. They speak of jagged cinder cones, deep basins, and perpetual snows. It sounds like spectacular country —the land between Mexico City and the Gulf Coast—and it is.

FLANKED BY VOLCANOES, the tiny village of San Simeon Xipetzingo, left, sits near majestic Popocatepetl and ragged Ixtaccihuatl. The hamlet is off Highway 136, near Apizaco. There are no tourist facilities, no paved streets—simply magnificent scenery. Popocatepetl, Ixtaccihuatl, and Malinche all are visible from Cholula, top left, just west of Puebla. Popo thrusts mightily above clouds and cornfields west of Puebla, right, creating a visual stereotype of Mexico that nevertheless is breathtaking in its beauty.

...Natural Wonders

EARLY MORNING in the mountains northeast of Puebla, and the sun throws the western flank of Malinche, below, into bold silhouette. At right, Popocatepetl exists in all the magnificence of its reality. It does not brood; it does not loom; it does not tower. It simply is there. Low haze is caused by the winter burning off of cornfields in preparation for spring planting.

Popocatēpetl
Pronounced Popo-ka-tay-peddle; also called Popo; name means smoking mountain. Smooth, classical pyramid form; peak thrusts above clouds, glistens with snow year-around. Elevation 17,887 feet.

Ixtaccíhuatl
Pronounced Ish-tok-zee-waddle; name means sleeping woman. Ragged slopes; top looks blasted off; peak usually snow covered, often obscured by clouds. Elevation 17,343 feet.

Malinche
Pronounced Moll-*inch*-ay; named after Cortes' Indian mistress. Long, gradual slopes rising from surrounding plain; usually no snow or clouds at peak; squat, brooding silhouette. Elevation 13,690 feet.

WHICH VOLCANO IS WHICH?
Between Mexico City and Puebla, as well as eastward of the latter, there are fine views of the plateau's principal volcanoes. Each peak has definite physical characteristics, though local inquiry may lead to a variety of answers as to which is which.

PUEBLA
Talavera Tiles and a Secret Convent

An overnight stop between Mexico City and either Veracruz or Oaxaca, Puebla is known as the city of tiles because of its liberal use of Moorish and Persian ceramics. Churches and private residences, store fronts and fountains are embellished with polychrome adornments that give the city and its surroundings a unique sparkle and color.

PUEBLA'S GRAND PLAZA is flanked by its tile-domed cathedral and by blocks-long portales *harboring excellent restaurants and shops. Since Puebla is a hub, a crossroads between Mexico City and points east, downtown traffic—and the din it creates—is tremendous (calm scene at right was photographed early on a Sunday morning). Driving in this city can be a terrifying experience for a newcomer, owing to the crush of automobiles and buses, the narrow streets, the complex street naming system. Most east-west arteries are called avenues; those running north-south are designated streets. Added to this is a sub-designation whereby some streets are termed* poniente *(west) and other* oriente *(east). And the custom of changing a street's name every few blocks adds spice to the stew. It's little wonder that even long-time residents can occasionally become confused.*

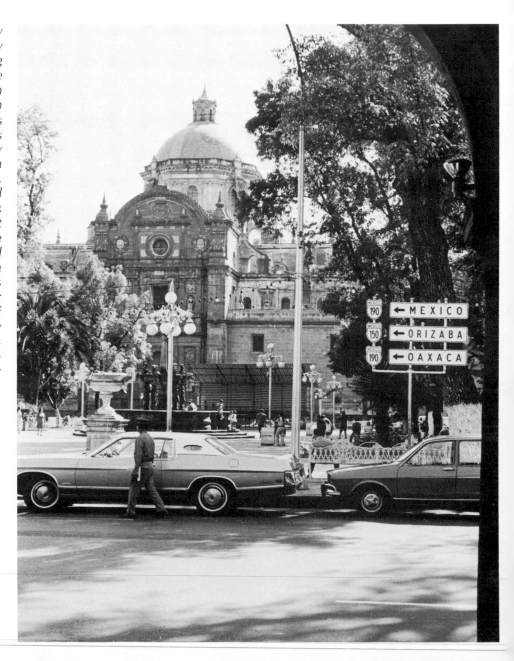

HANDPAINTED PLATES can be personalized with a name, above left, before being glazed and fired at a tile factory. Though the word "factory" is commonly used for the places that produce tile and onyx objects, the operation is usually a family-operated business employing no more than a dozen workers. Above right, pots and pitchers dry in the sun, waiting to be glazed. At left, visitors examine a religious painting in Puebla's Secret Convent of Santa Monica, a convent that continued to operate in secrecy despite religious persecution that began after 1850.

CENTER OF COLONIAL ARCHITECTURE, Cholula is said to have a church for every day of the year. Though there may not be quite that many, it does seem that the eye cannot move without falling on several at one time. Their numbers are probably due to the fact that during pre-Conquest times there were hundreds of Indian shrines and temples in the area, which the Spaniards offset with Christian structures. Church of San Francisco Acatepec, below is encrusted with beautiful Talavera tile. (Talavera is a type of ceramic work introduced by Spanish craftsmen brought from Talavera, Spain, shortly after the Conquest.) Interior, left, is a riot of carved cherubs, angels, and other lavish baroque ornamentation. Cholula is nine miles west of Puebla.

TILED DOMES of Puebla area sparkle in the sun. At lower left, Church of San Miguel, Huejotzingo; lower right, Church of Santa Maria Tonanzintla; below, Sanctuary of Los Remedios, Cholula. The latter church was constructed by the Spanish atop an Indian pyramid covered over with earth, left. The entire archaeological site is being restored as a national treasure.

The aroma of coffee is heady stuff, and the rapid rhythm of the marimba weaves in and out of the overlying sound of clattering streetcars and rapid-fire Spanish. The feeling is half Calypso, the mood half Spanish; but Veracruz is pure Mexican. Though tourism is neither promoted nor desired, this city on the gulf—where Cortes began his march to the Aztec capital—is friendly to anyone who is at all receptive to its noisy charm.

VERACRUZ
A Ten-Hour Coffee Break
to a Marimba Beat

SOCIAL LIFE and a good part of the business day center around the coffee house, where drinking of the strong brew has developed into a fine ritual. Waiter brings glass on a saucer and waits for you to put sugar into it, then pours thick, black coffee until you tell him to stop. You bang on glass with a spoon, and a white-jacketed boy fills it to the top with scalding milk. Veracruz is the sound of snarling coffee grinders, opposite, and steaming brewers, left.

. . . Veracruz

WATERFRONT SCENE looks like classic Navy recruiting poster, as sailor and friend admire visiting student ship. Across harbor broods the fortress of San Juan de Ulua, a grim, dank structure built for protection against pirates and once used as a prison. Tourist attractions are few in Veracruz, which, beneath the surface, is very much like old Spain in its customs. Mexicans refer to it as one of the last pockets of Spanish culture.

SUNDAY AFTERNOON on the Malecon (waterfront) brings out strollers, below, vendors of trinkets, and sellers of snacks. Families and young singles walk leisurely up and down until dusk, then wander over to the central plaza, two blocks away, to listen to the itinerant marimba bands. Left, musicians hustle their instruments across the street while an aged streetcar clanks by.

Little things speak of a country's character

The posters and the guidebooks and the colorful releases turned out by the tourist office glowingly describe one Mexico—the happy land whose surface is viewed by the short-term visitor. But to be understood, Mexico must be *seen*, not just looked at. It is a complex of layers, all made up of seemingly insignificant items, but each of which spells out a total way of life.

MEXICO IS a naked light bulb hanging from a hole in the ceiling of an otherwise well-appointed hotel room. Mexico is fruit stacked in the market in balanced pyramids reminiscent of the ceremonial structures of pre-Spanish cultures. Mexico is beautifully decorated skulls for Day of the Dead, a holiday when the Mexican laughs at death . . . and at life.

MEXICO IS a wall whose top is studded with the wicked points and jagged edges of broken glass, a sharp testimonial to the living paranoia of a once-exploited people. Mexico is the ever-present symbol of the country's leading political party, marked with a large "X" for the benefit of illiterate voters.

Forgetting Me is Your Loss

Some of the most ingenious messages in Mexico are found not printed in the news media but painted on the front bumpers of trucks. Every truck driver seems to consider himself to be a poet and his vehicle to be an animated extension of his personality. The majority of such inscriptions are religious in nature:

- *I drive and God guides me*
- *On the road God is my guide*
- *A prayer for a happy return*
- *Faith in God and forward*
- *God, me, and luck*

Another favorite type of epigram is that naming the truck, the driver, or both:

- *Magician of the highway*
- *The old wolf*
- *Martyr of Capricorn*
- *Vagabond of life*

Perhaps the most amusing apothegms are those that speak of unrequited love or are wondrously cryptic:

- *Beggar for love*
- *Even if you make me cry*
- *The treacherous blow*
- *Heart of stone*
- *Forgetting me is your loss*
- *I am that one*
- *River of life*
- *What the wind brings*
- *The smell guides me*

LA VENTA
From Out of a Swamp, the New World's First Civilization

In the teeming city of Villahermosa, capital of the steaming state of Tabasco, there is an incredible park that re-creates a site once inhabited by the Olmecas, one of Middle America's oldest civilizations. When the archaeological zone of La Venta, a marshy area in Veracruz, was threatened by oil exploration some years back, the site was moved bodily to Villahermosa, where it now forms a unique outdoor museum.

TWENTY-TON HEAD reposes in sightless serenity as visitors and civilizations come and go. Facial features are negroid; the football-type of headgear is believed to have been worn for ceremonial ball games. The leaf-strewn path winds through humid jungle, every turn offering a new thrill, a new marvel in the stone jaguars, monkeys, fish, owls, kings, and warriors that were created without metal tools. Since setting is at the marshy edge of a lake, insect lotion and sturdy shoes are invaluable for the visitors.

AQUILINE-NOSED, bearded man, left, called Uncle Sam by archaeologists, is a puzzle to scientists since other Olmec figures are characterized by broad, flat noses. Above, head deformation by binding tender cranium of infants was practiced as a beauty aid. At top, beautifully carved slab with monkey-faced man sitting cross-legged is presumed to have been a ceremonial altar.

PALENQUE
Jungle Tomb of the Maya Jade King

Fog lies heavy between the jungled hills, muffling the cries of birds and monkeys that live on the edges of this ancient Maya city. The deep Chiapas forest has been beaten back from the road to Villahermosa, but it reaches out hungrily toward the ruins as if eager to reclaim those venerable temples and pyramids brought to light by modern man.

"THE RUINED CITY becomes a kind of obsession," noted one archaeologist, after having explored Palenque's Great Palace and Observatory, opposite. The Crypt, above—discovered at bottom of a steep, rubble-filled stairway in the Pyramid of the Inscriptions, right— contained bones of a priest-king, jade, and stucco heads. The artifacts, as well as a re-creation of the tomb, are on exhibit at the National Museum of Anthropology in Mexico City. The 8-ton limestone slab covering sarcophagus is carved in beautiful relief.

Mexico

Survival of an

THE FORCES OF NATURE are constantly at work in Mexico's southern country. In few places is the influence of the land on its people so apparent. Variety and contrast are powerfully evident in Oaxaca. Its northern landscape is dry and flinty, the sun harsh, glaring off the baked earth. The ground is scarred, worn by the corrosive forces of man and eaten by the erosive forces of weather and time. Supporting few people, this land has been overworked to the point of near-barrenness.

Closer to the provincial capital, the face of the earth is split by great canyons and deep valleys. Foothills jumble and tumble against one another. In the dry season they are textured gold; when the rains come they are transformed into green velvet. Their slopes are stitched by crisscrossing paths, miniature terraces worn by countless generations of cattle whose legs must surely be shorter on one side than on the other from a lifetime of hillside grazing. Fields of greenish blue agave wait, bristling, to be processed into mezcal, the nectar of the south. Stolid and enduring, Oaxaca's Mixtecs and Zapotecs are as weathered in body as the rocks that lie long exposed to the sun, as sharp in spirit as the spines of the agave.

The Isthmus of Tehuantepec is dry country, flat-as-a-pancake country near the Pacific coast. Desiccating winds rage across this pinched waist of Mexico. As open as her land, the thick-waisted Tehuana is as independent as the gusts that blow over the region.

The rolling hills heave up into mountains that reach the chilly altitudes of Chiapas and stretch into Guatemala's highlands. This high sierra nurtures a man as carefree as the sky over his head, as sparklingly exuberant as the sun's rays. Contrasting sharply is the cautious, lowland Maya, who is unassuming and withdrawn, shy as the creatures that share his forests.

South
Ancient Outlook

MONTE ALBAN ▲ Oaxaca ▲ MITLA

Tehuantepec

San Cristóbal de las Casas

Tuxtla Gutierrez

Comitán

MEXICO

GUATEMALA

GULF OF TEHUANTEPEC

Tapachula

PACIFIC OCEAN

N

▲ Archaeological zone

0   50   100   150
Miles

SATURDAY IS MARKET DAY, and the market building as well as streets around are jammed with people, produce, pigs, and piles of pottery. Long before dawn, Indians from outlying mountain villages descend on Oaxaca for their big day in the city, wares piled high on their backs or roped to sleepy burros, which are left to doze for the day in a burro parking lot.

For some of their warmest memories of Mexico, many travelers are grateful to Oaxaca. Southern Mexico would be blessed many times over if it had only this provincial capital, with its fantastic baroque churches, its marvelous Indian market, its one-of-a-kind archaeological museum. But add to this the primitive beauty of the countryside, the wealth of Zapotec-Mixtec ruins, the villages rich in native crafts, the wonderfully earthy people, the brilliant fiestas, and it is little wonder that even Mexicans proclaim *Viva Oaxaca! No hay otro*—there is no other.

ZAPOTEC Indians hurrying from market pause in central plaza, right. Around the Zocalo are shaded arcades where voluble rug peddlers and jewelry hawkers thrust their goods at ear-weary patrons of sidewalk cafes. Five blocks north of the plaza is venerable Santo Domingo Church, above, whose walls and ceilings are covered with incredible high-relief polychrome sculpture.

BLACK POTTERY of Oaxaca is famous world-wide, the best being made in purest Indian tradition in the village of San Bartolo Coyotepec, right. Pieces are hand-formed, fired in pit kilns with covered vents, which imparts the smoky metallic finish, then carefully hand-burnished. A Zapotec woman, Dona Rosa, has become a legend among Coyotepec potters; her work is highly prized by collectors and is found in several museums.

Craft Towns of Oaxaca

Like the Guadalajara and Michoacan areas, Oaxaca is a region possessing a rich assortment of native crafts and popular arts. The city of Oaxaca has weavers who produce fine tablecloths, napkins, blouses, and dresses. There is production of carved wood images, masks, and combs. Onyx and marble are worked into boxes, ashtrays, and paperweights. Following are some of the other chief folk art centers in the state:

San Bartolo Coyotepec. Black smudged pottery (see photo above), animal figures, clay whistles.

Santa Maria Atzompa. Clay animals, dolls, Nativities, green-glazed pottery.

Ocotlan. Polychrome incense burners, human figures in clay, pottery.

Tehuantepec. Molded dolls, ceramic water coolers and jars, gold filigree, fiber and twine hammocks.

Juchitan. Black clay ware, water jars, embroidered blouses and skirts.

Yalalag. Blouses, sashes, silk rebozos, cast-silver crosses.

Etla. Gold filigree earrings, necklaces, bracelets, brooches, straw figures.

Ejutla. Machetes and daggers, tin picture frames and toys.

Tlaxiaco. Woven baskets, animals, hats, bird cages.

Santo Tomas Jalieza. Woven sashes, handbags, serapes.

San Antonio. Embroidered blouses.

Mitla. Woven headdresses, rebozos, serapes, belts, sashes, pottery.

Teotitlan de Valle. Serapes.

CROWNING GLORY of women of the towns of Tehuantepec and Juchitan is their magnificent gowns. The floral patterns are hand-embroidered on velvet; the delicately fluted petticoat is starched lace. Heavy gold chains and coins set off the festive costume and give evidence of family wealth. Tehuanas are noted for their sagacity in business dealings and for their straightforwardness and frankness. As one local male described them: "They are warm, open people. But if you betray their trust, you might as well leave town, because in their eyes you are dead." Between Tehuantepec and Oaxaca City are the Zapotec ruins of Mitla, above, dating from 500 A.D.

MONTE ALBAN
Ancient City Atop the Sacred White Mountain

The feeling that hits you first, and persists, even while you're crawling bent over into a dark tomb, is one of awe at the immensity of the place. Everything is so spread out, the sky so vast. As you cross the courtyard and climb stone steps to a temple that looks over the sweeping highlands you feel that man on earth is small, yet somehow significant.

CURIOUSLY CROUCHING MAN is one of several danzantes *(dancers) that delight the eye in a small court in Monte Alban's* danzante *group. Ancient figures carved in low relief on stone slabs by Zapotecs have facial features resembling those found in the Olmec culture, which existed earlier on Mexico's Gulf Coast (see page 214). In the state of Oaxaca there are today some 300,000 Indians who still speak the Zapotec language. The Zapotecs are also believed to have built Mitla, Yagul, Etla, and Xoxo, only a few of the hundreds of ruin sites in Oaxaca.*

CENTRAL TEMPLE SITE is situated on a north-south axis; view at left is from south platform looking northward. Just beyond the last structure at far end of the immense central plaza is Tomb 7, a mausoleum that contained gold jewelry, jade carvings, and alabaster and crystal bowls. (The treasures are on display at the Regional Museum in Oaxaca City.) Building in foreground nearest south platform is divided by a tunnel with a curious slit at the top believed to have been used for astronomical observations.

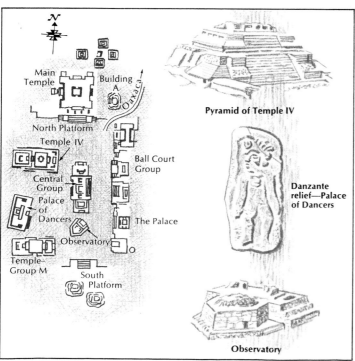

Pyramid of Temple IV

Danzante relief—Palace of Dancers

Observatory

MONTE ALBAN—SACRED CAPITAL OF THE ZAPOTECS
Entire archaeological zone spreads over more than 15 square miles. Area shown in plan, left, is main ceremonial center constructed atop an artificially leveled mountain.

OVERWHELMING VASTNESS is the feeling that prevails as you gaze across the ruins and down into the Valley of Oaxaca 1200 feet below. Massive stellae —stone slabs—atop platform at left, and at the foot of the main temple, below, are decorated with a form of hieroglyphics which have still not been deciphered and which are different from those of other pre-Columbian cultures.

The paseo is where boy meets girl in the Spanish tradition

On Saturday night in virtually every Mexican town, lights in the central plaza flicker on, the local band strikes up, and a charming courting ritual begins. Around the plaza saunter groups of girls and groups of boys, reserved but ever optimistic, timorous but ever hopeful.

EYE CONTACT IS BRIEF and a little hesitant the first few times as girls circle the plaza in one direction, boys in the other. There is a great deal of self-conscious giggling and good-natured horseplay, all under the watchful eye of parents and other relatives who sit on benches, gossip, and remember their own younger days.

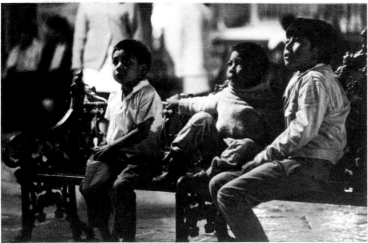

AT THE RIGHT MOMENT, a boy asks a girl to walk with him, or he simply joins her, and if all is well they break away from their groups and stroll around together, above. It is not uncommon for a proper young man to ask permission of the girl's parents to sit next to her, and sit they may for the entire evening without exchanging two words. When the small fry aren't tearing about, screeching in happy abandon, they pause enthralled by the band, left.

CHIAPAS HIGHLANDS
Pagan Rites in the Land of the Jaguar

MAGNIFICENCE MEETS THE EYE everywhere in the near-Guatemalan high country of Chiapas. At an altitude of a mile and a half, the crystal-clear air has an edge to it—a clean freshness unlike anything breathed in the flat lands. Below, several Chamula Indians pause for a rest on the rim of a sweeping valley, the men in white, the women in black. Opposite, a man and his dog wend their way home from the sugarcake cemetery of San Cristobal de las Casas, oldest Spanish city in Chiapas.

Tuxtla Gutierrez, capital of the state of Chiapas, is a tidy, businesslike city surrounded by tobacco and coffee plantations. Passing through it, the Pan American Highway continues west and south into Central America. Only a few hours from the capital are some of the most remote and least visited parts of Mexico—the highlands of Chiapas—close to Guatemala both geographically and culturally and little changed since the time of the Conquest.

SHUT OFF from the rest of southern Mexico, San Cristobal de las Casas (usually called simply Las Casas) is set gemlike in a 7,000-foot-high basin right on the Pan American highway before it winds into Guatemala. At right, a reminder of colonial days, El Carmen Arch spans Hidalgo Avenue, a cobbled street with two strips of flat paving blocks, the reason for which no one seems to know. The nearest large town is Tuxtla Gutierrez, 60 miles to the west.

Huisteco   Chamula   Zinacanteco

HOW TO TELL A CHAMULA FROM A ZINACANTECO FROM A HUISTECO Along the roadways and in the marketplace of Las Casas, three types of Indians are commonly seen. Huistecos wear patched white shirts; baggy trousers; perky hats with up-tilted brims. Chamulas wear heavy white or black ponchos tied with a leather band; white headcloths; peaked straw hats. Zinacantecos have short trousers; pink and white striped overblouses; tassled kerchiefs; flat straw hats with ribbons.

MAGIC AND WITCHCRAFT are blended with strange forms of Christianity in the lives of the highland Indians. During a pagan celebration that includes firewalking, participants race around the plaza of San Juan Chamula, above, yelling wildly and waving smoking incense burners prior to entering the church. Thoroughly relaxed celebrant below has drunk deeply of comiteco, a local liquid fire made from sugar cane.

The Lacandons: Jungle Survivors of a Vanished Civilization

Last of the pure Maya, and very proud of the fact, the mild Lacandons dwell in isolated jungle communities bordering the rivers and lakes of tropical Chiapas. They are a polygamous people, several wives living together with one husband under one roof. They make their simple apparel from cloth obtained from infrequent visitors or wear Western garb. In religious ceremonies they prefer a pre-Hispanic article of dress that has survived intact—a long, bark-cloth tunic made by pounding the bark of the *majugua* tree.

Periodically the Lacandons hold propitiatory rites to their ancient deities to request rain or a cure for sickness, the adult men gathering to pray, sing, and drink a beverage made from bark of the *balche* tree and wild honey. Images of the gods are molded from clay. When they lose their power through age, they are broken and new ones are created.

The Lacandons have great respect for Gertrude Blom, an anthropologist and tireless worker who spends a great part of her time in the jungle bringing canned foods, medicines, and gifts to the Indians.

"LIVING RELIEFS," Lacandon Indian profiles, below right and opposite, are reflected in stone sculpture from Yaxchilan, left, a ceremonial center of the ancient Maya. A ruined city larger than Palenque, Yaxchilan lies on the Usmacinta River near the Guatemala border, accessible only to the most adventurous. The Lacandons make annual pilgrimages there, believing that the old gods still reside in the ruins.

ARROW'S FLIGHT is watched intently by two Indians, above. A gentle people, the Lacandons use such weapons only for hunting monkeys or other deep-jungle creatures. Mahogany dugout canoes, left, are their chief mode of travel along the rivers and lakes in western Chiapas and Guatemala. Most dwellings are thatched huts without walls, because of the jungle heat. Remnants of a far-distant past, the surviving Lacandons number 300, are threatened by encroaching settlers and logging interests.

The Yucatan
Mystery Land

THE EARLY MORNING AIR is cool in Merida's main plaza. Breathing it deeply, a taxi driver discusses with a policeman a recent political address. "Someone is always making a speech," he says. "Too much talk means trouble." In a patch of sun on the southeast corner of the square stands a group of pieceworkers. Carpenters, waiters, and dishwashers, they meet each morning to exchange news on job openings. Happily deciding that the day has nothing better to offer, several stroll across the street to El Louvre for coffee. They seat themselves comfortably at a marble-topped table under a hand-lettered sign that reads: *"No tirar papeles ni escupir en el piso y las paredes"*: Don't throw papers or spit on the floor and walls.

At mid-morning a tourist in the Villahermosa airport wipes perspiration from his forehead and holds his watch to his ear. There are three clocks in the waiting room. One says 3:30, another 8:55, the third 9:25. The man's watch reads 10:15. He confronts the attendant at the airlines desk. "But when does the nine-thirty flight from Mexico City arrive?" he asks, desperately. The attendant lifts one shoulder, smiles, and consults a scrap of paper attached to a clipboard. "Around noon, senor," he answers.

By mid-afternoon the heat at Chichen Itza presses down like a weight. Guides and visitors sprawl on the shady side of a pyramid. Raising his hands to let air circulate through the wet patches under his arms, a man looks as if he is exhorting the ancient gods of the Maya.

Late in the afternoon a breeze rustles the palm trees on Cozumel. A Mexican couple watches the setting sun from the dining terrace of a luxury hotel at water's edge; they toss bits of bread to fish suspended in the crystal water below, who ignore the offering. A waiter leans over and whistles at the water. "They are taking a nap," he says.

Peninsula
of the Maya

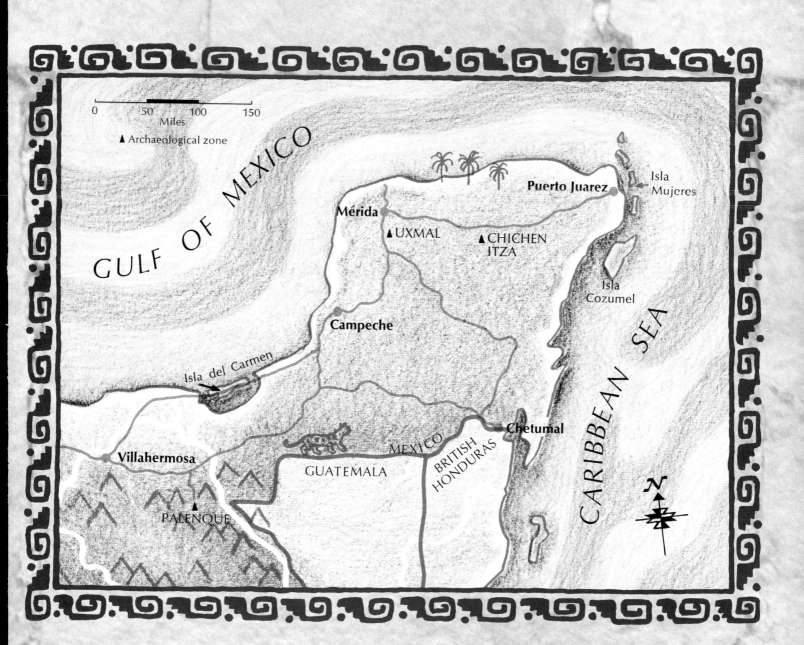

0   50   100   150
Miles

▲ Archaeological zone

GULF OF MEXICO

Puerto Juarez

Isla Mujeres

Mérida

▲ UXMAL

▲ CHICHEN ITZA

Isla Cozumel

Campeche

Isla del Carmen

CARIBBEAN SEA

Chetumal

Villahermosa

GUATEMALA

MEXICO

BRITISH HONDURAS

PALENQUE

N

OLD AND NEW are successfully combined in cluster of structures close by Campeche's waterfront, adjoining the government palace. Contemporary shapes of the acoustic shell, right, repeat forms and schemes of the city's old forts, moats, and walls. Lighthouse in background is actually one spire of a former church that is now a public library. This is a sea-going town. The taste of salt is in the air, the sound of the sea on the wind. This is an old town. Streets are narrow, faced with tired wooden houses with tall wooden doors and heavy iron grillework. Though friendly, the people of Campeche are somewhat wary, perhaps a throwback to the days when the city was sacked frequently by ocean-going freebooters.

CAMPECHE
A Quick-Paced Present Blended with a Piratical Past

There's no night life to speak of, unless you count the taut activity at the local pool hall. The few curio shops along Aleman Avenue are stuffed with dusty turtle shells, tarnished jewelry, and bottle openers with deer foot handles. Campeche is no tourist town, but to anyone who loves the sea, its mood is contagious.

BEACHED TRAWLERS, their hulls exposed for cleaning at low tide, left, look as if they had been fired on by the cannons of San Miguel fort. San Miguel, high on a hill overlooking Campeche, has a moat and drawbridge, houses an arms museum containing pirate artifacts, Spanish muskets, and crossbows. It and Saint Francis, above, are two of seven forts connected by walls circling the old part of town.

UXMAL
A Magician and Incredible Architecture

When you first spot the magnificent architecture from the Merida road, you feel your pulse quicken, and when you roam from the Governor's Palace to the Temple of the Magician, you feel privileged. Adjectives such as "beautiful" or "splendrous" come to mind, but so enthralling is this archaeological site that you experience it silently, subdued by its perfect harmony.

MAJESTY AND GRANDEUR are manifest in Governor's Palace and Pyramid of the Magician, opposite and left. Fantastic stone detail, above, from Nunnery Quadrangle represents faces of the rain god, Chac (for best effect hold picture at arm's length). Jaguar throne, top of page, is in front of the Governor's Palace. Here, a single handclap produces a sharp, musical echo that sets into flight thousands of swallows that nest in the Palace.

...Uxmal

PYRAMID OF MAGICIAN, also called Pyramid of the Dwarf, has five temples, built on top of one another over a period of three centuries. So terrifyingly steep and narrow are the steps leading to the temple on top that a chain is necessary as a reassuring handhold, going up or coming down. As one writer has said, it is as if the Maya architects had remembered the mountain peaks where the gods had been worshipped in the hazy past.

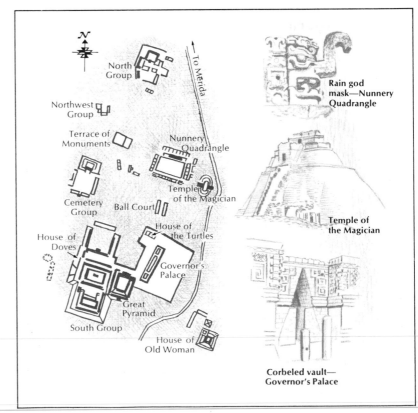

Rain god mask—Nunnery Quadrangle

Temple of the Magician

Corbeled vault— Governor's Palace

UXMAL—MAYA CITY IN THE YUCATAN

In this 250-acre archaeological zone, most of the structures are in the Puuc, or hill, style—decorations are largely in the friezes on the upper portions of buildings. Uxmal is 60 miles south of Merida, capital city of Yucatan.

ENORMOUS NUNNERY QUADRANGLE is a complex of four massive buildings facing inward on a grassy courtyard, each decorated with ornate stone latticework, masks of the rain god, human heads, and feathered serpents. The name Nunnery derives from the fact that this group of buildings contains 88 rooms, though it is unlikely that they were used to house maidens.

MERIDA
All the Earmarks of a Contented City

The first tone of simplicity is set by the whitewashed trunks of the Indian laurel trees shading Calle Montejo and ringing Merida's central plaza. Another note is sounded in the city's easy-to-follow streets. Then there is the clean dress of the men and the women. It's a contented place, and, like the smiles on the faces of its citizens, straightforward and elemental.

EARLY MORNING in Plaza de la Constitucion. It is between coffees, and the air is still. Two ladies move toward the market, the sun reflecting white off their cotton huipiles. A man sits contentedly, observing as time flows around him. (To the ancient Maya, Heaven was sitting in the cool shade of the ceiba tree.) On the south side of the plaza is Casa de Montejo, a colonial building built in 1549 as the residence of Francisco de Montejo, a name encountered often in the Yucatan. The house is still occupied by descendants of the builder and is open to the public.

HORSE-DRAWN CARRIAGE rattles past Cepeda Peraza Park, below, a block north of main plaza. Park is near Merida's principal hotels and is a central taxi stand for the downtown area. Imposing mansion at left houses regional archaeological museum, was once residence of a General, then of a Governor. The grand structure is one of many such "palaces" built by Merida's henequen barons along Montejo Street.

Henequen: The peninsula's economy is all tied up in twine

Henequen is defined in the dictionary as a tough fiber. The definition gives no hint of how, in the 1900's, henequen created in the Yucatan a breed of barons as wealthy as the silver nabobs of San Francisco. After a long slump, the industry again booms, based on hundreds of thousands of acres of agave.

SPIKY, BLUE AGAVE prickles the countryside around Merida. One of Mexico's most prolific producers, the agave plant—also called maguey and century plant—yields not only sisal hemp but also tequila (page 64), pulque, mezcal, and fabric (page 144). The tough, spear-shaped leaves are cut and hauled by burro to a henequen crushing plant such as the beautiful old hacienda near Muna, right.

AGAVE LEAVES GO IN and henequen strands come out of a disfibradora (de-fibering plant), where the only sound is the rhythmic slapping of the big belts that drive the crushing gears, above. The fibers are hung in the sun to dry, then are shipped to one of the Yucatan's modern Cordemex factories where they are baled, right, and woven into carpeting, sacks, and twine. Giant machines, programmed by computer, weave endless rugs in intricate Indian patterns.

CHICHEN ITZA
Monumental Home of the Maya Serpent God

The glory of ancient days still lives at Chichen Itza in its remarkable city planning, its flawlessly designed ball court, its architecturally perfect Castillo, its astonishing observatory. At every turn it is apparent that here dwelt a masterful group of people, a race that was far ahead of its time.

FLAT LANDSCAPE of the Yucatan is punctuated dramatically by Chichen Itza's two tallest structures, opposite. The light building in the foreground, believed to have been an astronomical observatory, is called the Caracol (snail) because of its interior convoluted stairway. Beyond, in shadow, is the majestic Castillo, or castle, a nine-terraced pyramid nearly 100 feet high. Main stairway up the Castle, left, leads to the temple of Kukulkan, a god of the ancient city. Under steps is a door opening to a cramped inner staircase that ascends to a chamber containing a life-sized jaguar—with staring jade eyes— painted red. Near the Castle is the wall of skulls, above, a platform built to hold skulls of victims sacrificed as religious offerings.

... **Chichen Itza**

THOUSAND COLUMNS is name given to architectural complex surrounding the ornate Temple of the Warriors, below. Rattlesnake figure predominates at Chichen Itza, forms a balustrade flanking stairway to top of the main platform; two huge serpent columns are entrance to the temple, right. Great Ball Court, opposite, constructed more than eight centuries ago, was used for ancient team games. Object was to hit a small rubber ball through the stone ring, 20 feet above the level of the court, using only the knees, feet, or hips. The gleeful player who did so could claim the possessions of onlookers.

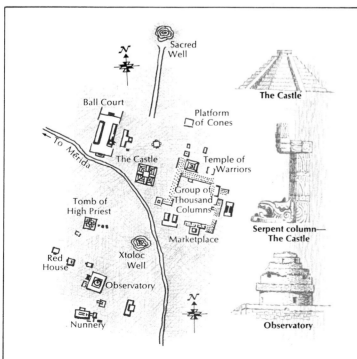

CHICHEN ITZA—"AT THE RIM OF THE WELL OF ITZA"
The name of this magnificent Toltec-Maya site, which covers six square miles, refers to the large natural well (cenote) near which the Itza people settled. The sacred cenote, north of the Castle, was believed to have been used for sacrificial purposes and quantities of treasures have been recovered from it. The archaeological zone of Chichen Itza is about 70 miles east of Merida.

THE CARIBBEAN
Islands in the Sun along an Unexplored Coast

CASTLE OF TULUM, the Yucatan's only ancient coastal Maya ruin, was probably seen by Juan de Grijalva, the Spanish explorer who sailed from Cuba along the Yucatan's east coast in 1518, the year before Cortes landed in Mexico. The walled fortress sits on a rocky bluff overlooking the Caribbean, southwest of Merida, in the territory of Quintana Roo. Sparkling sand and turquoise waters make these beaches some of the most beautiful in the world. There are no tourist facilities along the coast; however, the Mexican government is planning a long-term development of a huge resort complex at Concun, an area at the northeast tip of the peninsula, inshore from Isla Mujeres.

Along the Quintana Roo shore, the waves tumble onto some of the finest sand beaches to be found anywhere. Chicle trees and coconut palms sway in the offshore breezes, and Maya watchtowers thrust up from the flat land. Lying farther east than Chicago, the Yucatan's white Caribbean coast dips into an incredibly blue sea whose waters wash the edges of everyone's image of the idyllic tropical island.

A TROPICAL ISLE in every sense, Cozumel Island, left, is little changed from the time when Spanish explorers touched there on their voyages of conquest—except for several first-class resort hotels clustered at water's edge on the leeward shore. Cozumel's water is unbelievably clear, its sand incredibly white; it is a place where one could easily and happily become a beachcomber for life. Isla Mujeres—40 minutes north from Cozumel by air— moves at an even slower pace, is less touched by tourism. Its greatest activity is the sometimes daily arrival and departure of the cargo and passenger boat from the mainland, above.

SELECTED READINGS

A scholarly bibliography would include material published in Mexico and works printed abroad. Rather than claiming to be any kind of detailed reference source, the following listing comprises fairly recent books in English that are chiefly of a general nature and which are either published in the United States or readily obtainable in this country.

Books of General Interest

Berney, Henri-Maurice, Annaheim, Hans, Leuenberger, Hans. *Mexico.* Berne, Kummerly & Frey, 1969.

Brandenburg, Frank R. *The Making of Modern Mexico.* Englewood Cliffs, N.J., Prentice-Hall, Inc., 1964.

Camp, Andre, Elfer, Arpad. *The Mexico I Love.* New York, Tudor Publishing Co., 1968.

Covarrubias, Miguel. *Mexico South.* New York, Alfred A. Knopf, 1967.

De Mente, Boye. *Bachelor's Mexico.* Rutland, Charles E. Tuttle Co., 1967.

Dorner, Gerd. *Mexico.* Munich, Wilhelm Andermann Verlag, 1961.

Ewing, Russell C. *Six Faces of Mexico.* Tucson, The University of Arizona Press, 1966.

Foster, Lee. *Mexico: The Devil's Pinata.* Los Altos, Kauffman, 1973.

Hanf, Walter. *Mexico.* Munich, Wilhelm Andermann Verlag, 1967.

James, Daniel. *Mexico and the Americans.* New York, Frederick A. Praeger, 1963.

Johnson, William Weber. *Mexico.* New York, Time, Inc., 1966.

Leuenberger, Hans. *Mexico.* New York, Hill and Wang, 1967.

Lewis, Oscar. *Five Families.* New York, John Wiley & Sons, 1959.

———— *The Children of Sanchez.* New York, Random House, 1961.

Milne, Jean. *Fiesta Time in Latin America.* Los Angeles, The Ward Ritchie Press, 1965.

Murbarger, Nell. *30,000 Miles in Mexico.* Palm Desert, Desert Magazine Press, 1961.

Murray, Spencer. *Cruising the Sea of Cortez.* Palm Desert, Desert Magazine Press, 1963.

Norman, James. *A Shopper's Guide to Mexico: Where, What and How to Buy.* New York, Doubleday and Company, 1966.

Payne, Robert. *Mexico City.* New York, Harcourt, Brace and World, Inc., 1968.

Stephens, John Lloyd. *Incidents of Travel in Central America, Chiapas, and Yucatan.* New York, Dover Publications, 1963.

———— *Incidents of Travel in Yucatan.* New York, Dover Publications, 1963.

Vinding, Diana. *Mexico.* Chicago, Follett Publishing Co., 1968.

Zim, Herbert S. and Sonia Bleeker. *Mexico.* New York, Golden Press, 1969.

Specialized Subjects

Belden, L. Burr. *Baja California Overland.* Glendale, La Siesta Press, 1965.

Bernal, Ignacio. *3,000 Years of Art and Life in Mexico.* New York, Harry N. Abrams, Inc.

Best, Gerald M. *Mexican Narrow Gauge.* Berkeley, Howell-North Books, 1968.

Chan, Roman Pina. *A Guide to Mexican Archaeology.* Mexico City, Minutiae Mexicana, 1971.

Clark, Phil. *A Flower Lover's Guide to Mexico.* Mexico City, Minutiae Mexicana, 1968.

Coe, Michael D. *America's First Civilization.* New York, American Heritage Publishing Co., 1968.

Ellis, Allen R. and Phyllis T. *Baja By Air.* North Hollywood, Pan American Navigation Service, 1967.

Helfritz, Hans. *Mexican Cities of the Gods.* New York, Frederick A. Praeger, 1968.

Landis, Sam W. *A Hunter's Guide to Mexico.* Mexico City, Minutiae Mexicana, 1965.

Madsen, William and Claudia. *A Guide to Mexican Witchcraft.* Mexico City, Minutiae Mexicana, 1969.

Nicholson, Irene. *Mexican and Central American Mythology.* London, Paul Hamlyn, 1967.

———— *A Guide to Mexican Poetry.* Mexico City, Minutiae Mexicana, 1968.

Osborne, Harold. *South American Mythology.* Middlesex, Paul Hamlyn, 1968.

Padgett, Vincent L. *The Mexican Political System.* Boston, Houghton Mifflin Co., 1966.

Paz, Octavio. *The Labyrinth of Solitude.* New York, Grove Press, Inc., 1961.

Ramos, Samuel. *Profile of Man and Culture in Mexico.* Austin, University of Texas Press, 1969.

Romanell, Patrick. *Making of the Mexican Mind.* London, University of Notre Dame Press, 1952.

Senterfitt, Arnold. *Airports of Baja California.* P.O. Box 23166, San Diego, 1968.

_____ *Airports of Mexico & British Honduras.* P.O. Box 23166, San Diego, 1968.

Singer, Morris. *Growth, Equality, and the Mexican Experience.* Austin, University of Texas Press, 1969.

Smith, Bradley. *Mexico: A History in Art.* New York, Doubleday and Co., Inc., 1968.

Stierlin, Henri. *Living Architecture: Ancient Mexican.* New York, Grosset & Dunlap, 1968.

Stuart, George E., and Stuart, Gene S. *Discovering Man's Past in the Americas.* Washington, D.C., National Geographic Society, 1969.

Toor, Frances. *A Treasury of Mexican Folkways.* New York, Crown Publishers, Inc., 1947.

Vazquez, Pedro Ramirez. *The National Museum of Anthropology.* New York, Harry N. Abrams, 1968.

Wheeler, Margaret L. *A Bird Watcher's Guide to Mexico.* Mexico City, Minutiae Mexicana, 1967.

Wright, N. Pelham. *A Guide to Mexican Animals.* Mexico City, Minutiae Mexicana, 1965.

_____ *A Guide to Mexican Mammals and Reptiles.* Mexico City, Minutiae Mexicana, 1970.

Simpson, Lesley Byrd. *Many Mexicos.* Berkeley, University of California Press, 1967.

Smith, Justin H. *The Annexation of Texas.* New York, Barnes & Noble, 1941.

_____ *The War with Mexico.* 2 Vols. New York, Macmillan, 1919.

Soustelle, Jacques. *Daily Life of the Aztecs.* Stanford, Stanford University Press, 1962.

Turner, John Kenneth. *Barbarous Mexico.* Austin, University of Texas Press, 1969.

Vaillant, George C. *The Aztecs of Mexico.* Baltimore, Penguin Books, 1961.

Wolf, Eric R. *Sons of the Shaking Earth.* Chicago, Chicago University Press, 1959.

Historical Works

American Heritage. *Texas and the War With Mexico.* New York, American Heritage Publishing Co., 1961.

Bernal, Ignacio. *Mexico Before Cortes.* Garden City, N.Y., Doubleday & Company, 1963.

Blacker, Irwin R. *Cortes and the Aztec Conquest.* New York, American Heritage Publishing Co., 1965.

Cline, Howard F. *Mexico Revolution to Evolution.* London, Oxford University Press, 1962.

_____ *The United States and Mexico.* Cambridge, Mass., Harvard University Press, 1953.

De Fuentes, Patricia. *The Conquistadors.* New York, The Orion Press, 1963.

De Gomara, Francisco Lopez. *Cortes.* Berkeley, University of California Press, 1966.

Del Castillo, Bernal Diaz. *The Discovery and Conquest of Mexico.* New York, Noonday Press, 1956.

Henry, Robert. *Story of the Mexican War.* New York, Ungar, 1961.

Kibbe, Pauline R. *A Guide to Mexican History.* Mexico City, Minutiae Mexicana, 1964.

Leon-Portilla, Miguel. *The Broken Spears.* Boston, Beacon Press, 1969.

Leonard, Jonathan Norton. *Ancient America.* New York, Time, Inc., 1967.

Manje, Captain Juan Mateo. *Unknown Arizona and Sonora.* Tucson, Arizona Silhouettes, 1954.

Morley, Sylvanus Griswold. *The Ancient Maya.* Stanford, Stanford University Press, 1956.

Parkes, Henry Bamford. *A History of Mexico.* Boston, Houghton Mifflin Company, 1970.

Pourade, Richard F. *The Sign of the Eagle.* San Diego, Union-Tribune Publishing Co., 1970.

Prescott, William H. *History of the Conquest of Mexico.* New York, Bantam Books, 1964.

Recinos, Adrian, Goetz, Delia, and Morley, Sylvanus, G. *Popul Vuh.* Norman, University of Oklahoma Press, 1950.

Reed, John. *Insurgent Mexico.* New York, Simon and Schuster, 1969.

Guide Books

American Automobile Association. *Mexico and Central America.* Washington, D.C., American Automobile Association, 1973.

Carlson, Loraine. *Mexico: An Extraordinary Guide.* Chicago, Rand McNally & Co., 1971.

Cross, Cliff. *Baja.* North Palm Springs, 1971.

_____ *Guide to Mexico.* North Palm Springs, 1970.

_____ *Yucatan Peninsula.* North Palm Springs, 1971.

Ellis, Allen R. and Phyllis T. *Discovering Mayaland.* Glendale, The Arthur H. Clark Co., 1964.

Flandrau, Charles M. *Viva Mexico!* New York, Harper and Brothers, 1951.

Holiday Magazine. *Travel Guide to Mexico.* New York, Random House, 1968.

Liebes, Herman and Juanita. *Guide to Mexico.* Chicago, Rand McNally, 1961.

Nash, Joe. *A Guide to Mexico City.* Mexico City, Minutiae Mexicana, 1966.

Norman, James. *Terry's Guide to Mexico.* New York, Doubleday and Co., Inc., 1962.

Simon, Kate. *Mexico Places and Pleasures.* New York, Doubleday and Co., Inc., 1963.

Sunset. *Travel Guide to Baja California.* Menlo Park, Lane Books, 1971.

_____ *Travel Guide to Mexico.* Menlo Park, Lane Books, 1967.

Toor, Frances. *New Guide to Mexico.* New York, Crown Publishers, Inc., 1965.

Wilcock, John and Guest, Phyllis. *Arthur Frommer's Dollar-Wise Guide to Mexico.* New York, Frommer-Pasmantier Publishing Corp., 1968.

Wilhelm, John. *Guide to Mexico.* New York, McGraw-Hill Book Co., 1966.

Index

This book was printed and bound by Kingsport Press, Kingsport, Tennessee, from litho film prepared by Graphic Arts Center, Portland, Oregon. Body type is Optima; heads are Roberta and Optima, composed by Atherton's Advertising Typography, Inc., Palo Alto, California. Paper for pages is Sterling Enamel made by Westvaco, Luke, Maryland.

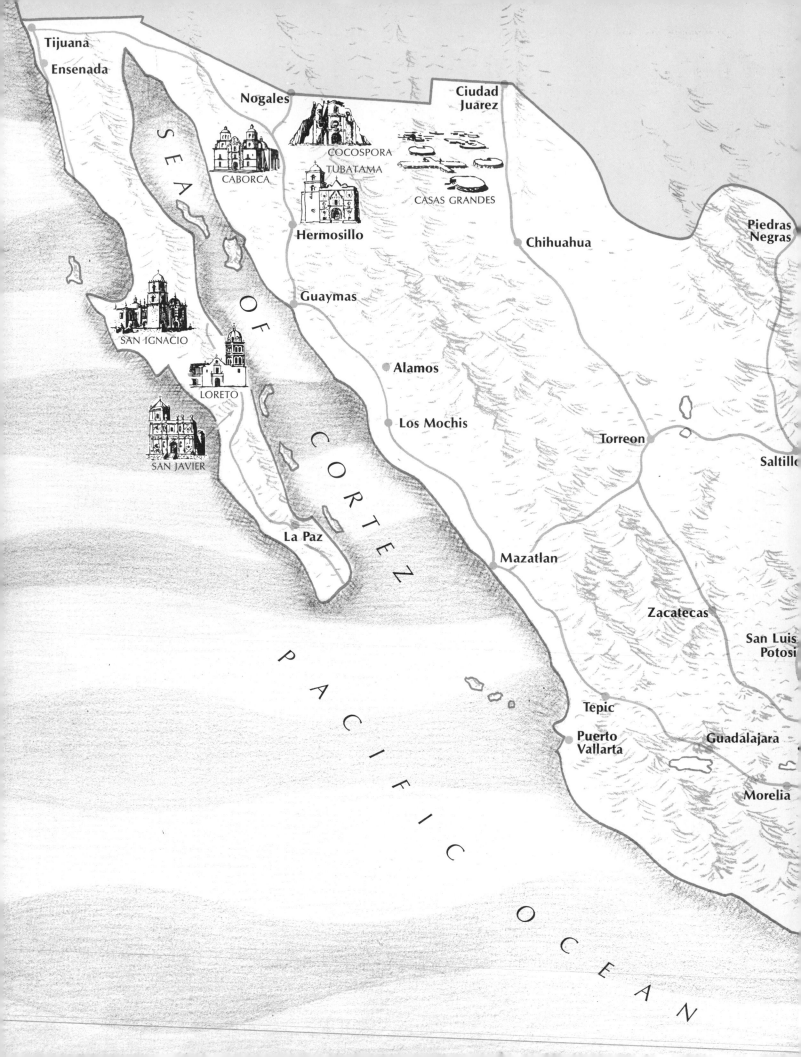

Tijuana

Ensenada

SEA OF CORTEZ

Nogales

COCOSPORA

TUBATAMA

CABORCA

Ciudad
Juarez

CASAS GRANDES

Piedras
Negras

Hermosillo

Chihuahua

Guaymas

SAN IGNACIO

LORETO

SAN JAVIER

Alamos

Los Mochis

Torreon

Saltillo

La Paz

Mazatlan

Zacatecas

San Luis
Potosi

Tepic

Puerto
Vallarta

Guadalajara

Morelia

PACIFIC OCEAN